THE JOURNAL OF FRANCOIS LAROCQUE

The Larocque narrative was printed by the Canadian Government in English in 1910, and in French in 1911. Aside from possible wandering Spaniards Larocque was the first white man to explore northern Wyoming.

The *Francois Larocque* is Number L-107 in Wright Howes' *U.S.-IANA.-1650-1950*.

THE JOURNAL OF FRANCOIS LAROCQUE

BY

FRANCOIS LAROCQUE

Ye Galleon Press

Fairfield, Washington

1981

Library of Congress Cataloging in Publication Data

Larocque, Francois Antoine.
    The journal of Francois Larocque.

    Originally published: Ottawa : Government Printing Bureau, 1910.
(Publications of the Canadian Archives ; no. 3) With new introd.
    "Bibliography by L.J. Burpee": p.
    Includes index.
    1. Northwestern States—Description and travel. 2. Indians of North
America—Northwestern States. 3. Crow Indians. 4. Fur trade—
Northwestern States. 5. Larocque, Francois Antoine. I. Title. II. Series:
Publications of the Canadian Archives ; no. 3.
F597.L32   1981   917.7'043   81-21836
ISBN 0-87770-262-4   AACR2

Of this book 498 copies were printed.

This is Copy Number 199 .

TABLE OF CONTENTS

INTRODUCTION

On December 20, 1803 the American troops marched into New Orleans, the French flag was lowered and the Stars and Stripes were raised. France ceded the Louisiana territory to the fledgling Republic of the United States. This historic action was definitive. However, the boundaries of the lands of Louisiana in the Treaty with France were not spelled out — they were not definite. The Spanish-claimed lands reached up north from Mexico with indefinite lines. President Adams conceded, because of Spanish discoveries and settlements, that the forty-second parallel of latitude be the northern boundary on the Pacific coast. The eastern boundary between Britain and the colonies was settled but the forty-ninth parallel in the West was not as yet set down in any treaty.

President Jefferson in February 1803 — six months before the Louisiana Purchase — moved Congress to appropriate funds for a Pacific expedition. In this unsettled situation, as to the boundaries of the Louisiana Purchase, Lewis and Clark Expedition wintered in 1804 at the Mandan village on the Missouri River.

In November of 1804 Monsieur Chaboillez, the *Bourgeois* in charge of the Assiniboine Department of the North West Company, sent a trading expedition south to the Missouri River to explore the fur-trade opportunities. The small group of six men, under Francois-Antoine Larocque, met the American Lewis and Clark Expedition at the Mandan village November 25, 1804 (November 27 in the Lewis and Clark Journals). After the second Larocque journey of 1805 to the Yellowstone River and after the reports of F.A. Larocque and Charles MacKenzie were sent to headquarters, the North West Company abandoned further attempts at trading in American lands.

The *Missouri Journal* (in two parts) and the Charles Mackenzie *Journal to the Mississouri Indians* (four parts) were written in the present form at the request of Roderick McKenzie, who planned a large scale account of the *Companie du Nord-Ouest*. Senator L.R. Masson obtained Roderick McKenzie's notes which were never printed, and included F.A. Larocque's and Charles Mackenzie's journals in his *Les Bourgeois de la Companie du Nord-Ouest*.

Francois-Antoine Larocque, (born between 1782-1785), a *Commis* (clerk) in the service of the North West Company, was conversant in French and English. He preferred writing in English. Abbe Morice described him as "a well-educated person, of great courage and fecund in deed." He was the son of Francois-Antoine Larocque, Sr. (born 1753 at Quebec) and Angelique Leroux. The younger brother Joseph Larocque was long associated with the X-Y Company and the North West Fur Company and advanced to be a chief-trader with the Hudson's Bay Company. Joseph Larocque was with John George McTavish when the North West Company negotiated the purchase of Astoria in 1813 and remained in the Columbia River area to 1817. In 1837 he went to France, and returned to Canada after a fourteen-year stay. He died at the Convent of the Grey Nuns at St. Hyacinthe in 1866. He continued his interest in the Pacific Northwest leaving his estate to found St. Joseph College at St. Paul on the Willamette in Oregon Territory.

Entering the service of the X-Y Company in 1801 as a clerk, Francois-Antoine was stationed at various times at Fort Alexandria, at the Churchill River factory at Montagne a la Bosse and Fort Assiniboine. In 1804 he made the journey to the Mandans and in 1805 to the Yellowstone River to the country of the Crow Indians. He retired from the fur-trade in 1815. He married Miss Cote, daughter of a Fort Michilimackinac merchant. They left only one son Alfred Larocque who married Emelie Berthelet, the daughter of Olivier Berthelet, a long-honored benefactor of the Providence Sisters of Montreal. Emelie's mother was Angelique Chaboillez. Of this Alfred and Emelie marriage ten children survived, one of whom was Alfred Larocque, the *Papal Zouave;* another was Therese Emelie (1856-1897) who married the Honorable J. Alderic Ouimet, Speaker of the House of Commons.

In 1815 Francois-Antoine retired from the North West Company. He left the West returning to Montreal and was elected a member of the *Beaver Club*. He then entered into an unfortunate business venture. He lived to an advanced age in the convent of the Grey Nuns at St. Hyacinthe in Montreal where he passed away.

The Larocque family had a long distinguished history of service to the Catholic Church of Quebec. A number of its members were nuns, priests and one was a bishop. Also besides Joseph Larocque of the Hudson's Bay Company and Francois-Antoine Larocque, the author of the *Missouri Journal* there were other Larocques (LaRocque) engaged in the fur-trade. The *Listes des Bourgeois* of the North West Company also list Antoine, Charles, Jacques, J.B. Sr., J.B. Jr., Joseph, Pascal and Pierre Larocque.

Edward J. Kowrach
Veradale, Washington
September 1981

THE

MISSOURI JOURNAL

BY

F. A. LAROCQUE[1]

CLERK OF THE NORTH-WEST CO.

1804-1805

Set off from Fort Assiniboine, at 2. P.M., for the Missouri with a trading equipment. We had nine horses, five of which were loaded with the Company's property. Our company consisted of Charles McKenzie, Bte. Lafrance, Wm. Morrison, Joseph Azure, Bte. Turenne, Alexis McKay and myself. Encamped about three miles from the Fort, near a small pond of stagnated water in order to wait for Morrison who had remained behind with one horse and load. He arrived an hour after: sent McKay to the Fort to fetch

1804
Nov. 11th

N.B.—*The Mississouri Indians: A Narrative of Four Trading Expeditions to the Mississouri, 1804-1805-1806,*Vol. I, pp. 315-353, Antiquarian Press Ltd., New York, 1960, of Mr. Charles Mac Kenzie was one the accounts requested by Roderick Mc Kenzie, of the North West Company, for his projected "Some Account of the Northwest Company," which never got printed. Senator L. R. Masson included this account in *Les Bougeois de la Compagnie du Nord-Ouest.* Charles Mac Kenzie's account of 1804-1805 duplicates much of F. A. Larocque's *Journal.* The notes following are identified as "C. Mac Kenzie" are additions amplifying Larocque's *Journal.*

[1] Mr. Francois-Antoine Larocque was a brother of Mr. Joseph Larocque, who occupied for many years a very prominent position in the North-West and Hudson Bay Companies. See: Tassé, *Les Canadiens de L'Ouest.*

Mr. F. A. Larocque was a man of good abilites, of great courage and energy. He was well read, studious and equally proficient in the use of the French and English languages, but he decidedly preferred the latter.

The life of an Indian trader had not for him the attractions it had for his brother; he soon left the North-West, came to Montreal and entered business, in which he was most unfortunate. He passed the last years of his life in close retirement and arduous study, and died, much advanced in years, in the Grey nunnery of St. Hyacinthe.

Mr. Larocque married a Miss Coté, the daughter of an independent North-West trader, and the sister of Mr. Jules Maurice Quesnel. He left only one son, Mr. Alfred Larocque, the father of Mr. Le Chevalier Larocque, ex-papal zouave; of Mr. Armand Larocque and of Mrs. Alderic Oimet, the wife of the Speaker of the House of Commons.

9

provisions for himself, which he had forgotten. Messrs. Chaboillez[2] and Henry came to see me; they remained with us a few hours, bid us farewell and departed.

. . . .

14th. Our course since leaving the fort has been west of south. Set off in a south south-west direction, but the plains being burnt, we changed our course north-west by west in order to find food for our horses, having been informed that the plains were not burnt in that direction. — Encamped at sunset at the last woods upon the second river of the Elk Head, having crossed the first river nearly at its source in the plains.[3] — Mr. McKenzie broke his gun.

15th. Removed our situation to about seven miles higher up the river, there being better food for the horses, and from whence the *traverse* of the plains is shorter to River *La Souris*, as it was impossible to get by day to that river from where we slept last night, as there is not a stick of wood in the intermediate space.

16th. Set off early in the morning and did not stop at all in the course of the day. Perceived the woods upon the *Souris* at sunset and arrived at them before dark, after having crossed a creek in the plains, called by the Indians "Deep River," from its being very deep in some places, where the water gathers and forms into lakes . . . . . The plains were burnt in many places.

. . . .

18th. Set off one hour and a half before day light, — walked hard till noon, when we arrived at the woods, — stopped one hour to refresh ourselves and horses, — resumed our course, still following the river and encamped upon it at sunset.

. . . .

19th. ....The plains being on fire to the south-west and the wind blowing from that quarter, brought such volumes of smoke as prevented us from seeing one hundred yards before us, so that we were forced to stop at a creek which lay in our way and which disemboges in the *Souris*, and there pass the night.

[2] Charles Mac Kenzie: "Charles [Jean-Baptiste] Chaboillez, one of the [wintering] partners of the North-West Company, then acting in the Department of the *Assinboine River*."

[3] C. Mac Kenzie: "we came to the *Dog Lodge*, a remarkable place which the Sioux warriors often frequent in their hostile excursions."

Francois Larocque

Went down the Creek and came to the river which we followed for an hour and a half; we again ascended the hills. The wind having shifted south, the weather was clear for about two hours, when it again veered to the south-west and we were involved in smoke, but not so thick as yesterday. 20th.

At 10 A.M., we stopped on a hill to look at a dark spot with the help of a spy glass; it appeared moving and we found it to be buffaloes. As we were moving off, we heard a number of people wooping and hollowing as Indians generally do when at war. Hills prevented us from seeing whom they proceeded from; we immediately unsheated our guns for defence, as we were certain that, if they were numerous enough, they would endeavour to pillage us of our goods, it being their fixed determination to prevent, as much as they can, any communication between their traders and the Missouri Indians, as they wish to engross that trade themselves. False alarm.

However, they soon appeared to the number of eight, and behaved very peaceably; they asked for a little tobacco, we gave them four inches to each and twenty rounds of ammunition among them all. As we were going off, one of them went before the horses and endeavoured to prevent them from passing, being, I suppose, displeased at not receiving more. He let his robe fall and put an arrow in his bow, as if to let fly at the horse; however, we soon got him to give way and went on. One of them followed us for about one mile, and, being questioned, said he wanted more tobacco. I refused giving him any, being very sorry they had got any at all.

They informed us that they were coming from the Missouri villages, where a great number of their nation, that is Assiniboines, had been and were on their way back, whom they said we would probably meet with them and likewise with a band of Knisteneaux who had also been there trading corn and horses.

Continued our journey and encamped at sunset on the side of a creek. The plains all burnt, excepting the spot on which we encamped. When it was dark, we tied our horses with long cords to pickets fixed in the ground, in order that they might not get away from us during the night; kept watch over them all night by turns, being apprehensive that some of these vagabonds had followed us to steal them.

11

22nd.   Prepared to set off, but two horses belonging to Lafrance and Azure are missing. Remained here the whole day to search for them but to no effect. — Killed a bull. At sunset removed a little higher upon the *coulée* to a better place for the feeding of our horses, where we kept them tied to pickets all night.

23rd.   Set off at break of day, taking the loads of the missing horses on Mr. McKenzie's horse and my own. — Found the Assiniboine road leading to the Missouri at 9 o'clock A.M.; — as mid-day passed one of their encampments, counted seventy-five fire-places; — passed two more encampments in the evening and stopped for the night by the side of a small lake around which, and no where else, there was grass for our horses. . . . .

24th. Set off at sunrise; two hours after, met with two of the Big Belly[4] Indians who were going hunting; they appeared well pleased to see us; I smoked a pipe with them and departed. At mid-day, saw the smoke of one of the Big Belly villages to the south of which we passed; at two, arrived at another of their villages where I enquired for Charbonneau,[5] (it being his usual place of residence,) and was informed by a Hudson's Bay man, who is there for the purposes of trade, that he was with some Americans, below the Mandan village, to whom he is engaged. Being unwilling to leave the Hudson's Bay man here alone to get the whole trade of this village, I got the horses unloaded and made a small equipment of goods which I gave in charge to Mr. McKenzie.

25th.   Left Morrison with Mr. McKenzie in the best lodge we could
He meets find, and proceeded to the Mandan villages with the remainder of
with Cap-
tain Lewis. the goods — excepting an equipment destined for the upper village of the Big Bellys — On the road thither, met with Captain Lewis, chief of the American party — with Jussiaume and Charbonneau — ; had about a quarter of an hour's conversation with him, during which he invited me to his house and appeared very friendly.

Arrived at the Mandan village at 3 P.M., entered the lodge of the Black Cat, the chief of the village, sent for the "Grand," the chief of the other Mandan village, gave them both a chief's clothing

---

[4] Gros Ventres nation

[5] René Jussomme, Touissant Charbonneau and his Shoshone Indian wife, Sacajawea, were hired by the American Expedition of Lewis and Clark.

Francois Larocque

and explained to them the motive of my coming &c. — gave a pipe of tobacco to all the grown men as usual; sent Azure and McKay with the Grand on the other side of the river with an equipment of goods in charge of Azure.

Lafrance traded 350 skins in wolves in kitts from the Indians of this village, he being the person to whom I gave this outfit in charge. The Indians appeared to be of a very thievish disposition. 26th.

Went over to see Azure, and what trade he had, which was about 250 plues. Returned to the Black Cat's. Captain Lewis returned from above and stopped at the lodge. — Spoke to Charbonneau about helping as interpreter in the trade to the Big Bellies; he told me that, being engaged to the Americans, he could not come without leave from Captain Lewis, and desired me to speak to him, which I did. Capt. Lewis told me that, as he had no business for Charbonneau but at times during the winter, he had no objections to his helping me upon certain conditions, which agreeing to, Charbonneau promised me he would come next morning. 27th.

The Black Cat went to dine with the Americans with two other chiefs, upon an invitation from Captain Lewis, who had also invited me, but, expecting Charbonneau, I declined going. 28th.

Still very bad weather which, as I thought, prevented Charbonneau from coming. In the evening the weather cleared, went to see what was the reason he did not come, — was very politely received by Captain Lewis and Clarke and passed the night with them. Just as I arrived, they were despatching a man for me, having heard that I intended giving flags and medals to the Indians, which they forbid me from giving in the name of the United States, saying that the Government looked upon those things as the sacred emblems of the attachment of the Indians to their country. As I had neither flags nor medals, I ran no risk of disobeying those orders, of which I assured them. 29th.
The "Lewis
& Clarke"
expedition.

They next called Charbonneau and gave him leave to come with me, but strictly enjoined not to utter a word to the Indians which might in any way be to the prejudice of the United States, or of any of its citizens, although I should order him to do so, "which," said they, turning to me, "we are very far from thinking you would."

13

Their party consists of 40 odd men besides themselves. and are sent by Government for the purpose of exploring the North West countries to the Pacific Ocean, so as to settle the boundary line between the British and the American territories; likewise to make it known to the Indians on the Missouri and adjacent country, that they are under the Government of the Big Knives, who will protect them and supply them with all their wants, as long as they shall behave as dutiful children of the Great Father, the President of the United States, &c., &c., — which has been the continual subject of their harangues to the Indians throughout the winter.

They showed me their passports and letters of recommendation from the French, Spanish and British Ministers at the city of Washington, which say that the object of their voyage is purely scientific and literary, and in no way concerning trade; desiring all persons under their respective Governments to aid and assist that party as much as in their power lies, in case they should be in want of anything in the course of their voyage. They have, likewise, letters of credit from the American Government for the payment of any drafts they should draw upon it.

They left Philadelphia in the Spring of 1803, came down the Ohio, passed the winter at the mouth of the Missouri, at St. Lewis, in the Illinois country. It took them the whole summer to come to the Mandans, at which place they arrived in October last. They made treaties of peace with all the Indian nations they saw on their road, excepting the Sioux, with whom they were very near coming to an engagement. They made presents of a flag, medal, chiefs clothing, tobacco, knives, beads and other trinkets to every chief of the Indian nation which they saw, but have not given a single shot of ammunition.

Free trade with the Indians. 30th.

They told me it was not the policy of the United States to restrain commerce, and fetter it as was the case when Louisiana belonged to the Spanish; that we and all the persons who should come in their territories for trade or for any other purpose, will never be molested by an American officer or commandant, unless his behaviour is such as would subject an American citizen himself to punishment. Nor will any trader be obliged to pay for permission to trade, as was formerly the case under the Spanish, as no exclusive priviledge will be granted. Every one will be free to trade after his own manner.

One thing that Government may do, as it has already done about Detroit and other places where opposition in trade ran high, is to have a public store well assorted of all kinds of Indian goods, which store is to be opened to the Indians only when the traders in opposition run to too excessive lengths; for the purpose of under selling them and, by that means, keep them quiet. No *derouine* to take place, no liquors to be sold, &c.[6]

In short, during the time I was there a very grand plan was schemed, but its being realized is more than I can tell, although the Captains say they are well assured it will.

Returned to the Mandans; Charbonneau got ready to come with me, but just as he was setting off, he received order to follow Captain Clarke, who was going with 25 men to join a party of Mandans and repulse some Sioux who killed a Mandan yesterday, and were supposed to be in the neighborhood. Went to see Azure and give him direction how to make the packs, as I intend to send to the fort very soon, having wherewith to load the Company's horses.

Captain Clarke's expedition did not succeed and Charbonneau joined me here this morning. Prepared to set off with him to settle the Upper Village of the Big Bellies, when Mr. McKenzie and an Hudson's Bay man arrived. We all set off together and slept at the Little Village in Mr. McKenzie's lodge. DECEMBER 1st.

Left this village in the morning with Charbonneau and Turenne with the Upper Village outfit, at which place we arrived at mid-day. Entered in the lodge of the White Wolf, a great chief and a well disposed Indian towards the Whites. Clothed him as a 2nd.

---

[6] C. Mac Kenzie: "Captain Lewis, with three interpreters, paid a visit to the *Gros Ventres* village....After haranguing the Indians and explaining to them the purport of his expedition to the westward, several of them accepted of clothing, but notwithstanding, they could not be reconciled to like these "strangers" as they called them.

" 'Had these Whites come among us,' said the chiefs 'with charitable views they would have loaded their 'Great Boat' with necessaries. It is true they have ammunition, but they prefer throwing it away idly than sparing a shot of it to a poor Mandane'....The American gentlemen gave flags and medals to the chiefs on the condition that they should not go to war unless the enemy attacked them in their villages."

chief and harangued him, &c.; he got a good bed made for us and we fixed our goods. Gave him 30 rounds ammunition, 3 knives, 1 awl, vermillion and a few beads.

. . . .

5th.   Snowing very hard, wind north-west. In the evening, my man went to see the Hudson's Bay trader and found him ready to set off with an Indian, having each a small bundle on their backs. He came and told me of it, upon which, I ordered him and Charbonneau to get ready, made a small equipment of goods into two parcels, got an Indian to guide them, and sent them in pursuit of the Hudson's Bay man who, not finding the Indians where they expected, returned. My people who were going met them, so they all returned together and arrived at eleven at night.

. . . .

13th.   Despairing to find the horses[7], got an old man to make a harangue, offering 30 balls and powder, 1 knife and a bit of tobacco to him who would find the horses and bring them back. Gave my landlord, the White Wolf, 50 balls and powder, 2 knives, 2 awls, ½ fathom of tobacco, 2 flints, 2 wormers and a little vermillion. Intending to set off to-morrow morning for the Fort, harangued him, &c., &c. Spoke to Charbonneau about his debt, telling that as he had two horses, he might send one in part payment, &c.; he consented, and early in the morning, I sent Morrison to Fort Mandan for the horse. Wrote a few lines to Captain Lewis and Mr. McKenzie.

14th.   Morrison arrived with Charbonneau's horse, brought a note from Captain Lewis. Sent Indians to seek the horses which had not yet been found, offered 40 rounds, 1 looking glass, 1 knife and a bit of tobacco, &c., — heard that the horses had been found and left at the little village below, — set off with Morrison to go and fetch them. Returned after dark and found Mr. Heney who was just arrived from Fort Assiniboine with two Indians. He brought a letter from Mr. Chaboillez which altered my plan as to going to the Fort; so that I will now pass the winter here.

---

[7] Lost and unsuccessfully "looked for" since several days.

Set off with Mr. Heney to go to the Americans; slept at Mr. McKenzie's.[8]

Arrived at Fort Mandan, being the name the Americans give to their Fort which is constructed in a triangular form, ranges of houses making two sides, and a range of amazing long pickets, the front. The whole is made so strong as to be almost cannon ball proof. The two ranges of houses do not join one another, but are joined by a piece of fortification made in the form of a demi circle that can defend two sides of the Fort, on the top of which they keep sentry all night; the lower parts of that building serves as a store. A sentinel is likewise kept all day walking in the Fort. *[16th. Fort Mandan. 17th.]*

We remained here all day. The Captain enquired a great deal of Mr. Heney concerning the Sioux nation and local circumstances of that country and lower part of the Missouri, of which they took notes . . . .

Slept at Mr. McKenzie and heard that 16 horses had been stolen at the Upper Village by the Assinboines. *[18th.]*

Ar   Arrived at my lodge; the report of so many horses having been stolen was confirmed, among which were 2 belonging to the Company, and 2 to Lafrance. — People buying horses; bought a stout mule for which I paid: 1 gun, 1 large axe, 1 awl, 1 looking glass, 1 fathom[9] Hudson's Bay red strouds, 1 fathom tobacco, 2 flints, 3 strings pipe beads, 300 balls and powder, 2 knives, 2 wormers, and a little vermillion. *[19th.]*

About sixty warriors set off to revenge upon the Assiniboines for stealing their horses. Took an inventory of the remaining goods here.

Sold an old gun to Turenne to help him to buy a horse; wrote to Mr. Chaboillez, and the people set off for the Assinboine River. Sent 6 pactons of furs containing 545 kitts, 57 wolves, 4 foxes, 7 beaver, 5 bags of corn and a horse. I kept two of the Company's horses here, being so poor and sore backed that they were not able to go to the Fort. Made Morrison remain to take care of them. *[20th.]*

. . . .

Hearing that there was a band of Indians hunting two days' *[26th.]*

[8] C. Mac Kenzie: "Report was in circulation that the company of Sir Alexander Mac Kenzie [the XY Company] had coalesced with the North-West Company both forming but one concern."

The Trade.

march off, sent Morrison to the Americans to fetch Charbonneau, in order to go to them, as I hardly get a skin when the Hudson's Bay trader is with me, as he understands and talks their language and is known by all the Indians; my getting skins at the Big Bellie's since my arrival was owing to my having such goods as pleased the Indians, i.e., strouds,[9] capotries, iron works, &c., which my opponent had not, but now that my trading goods are such as he has likewise, he gets nearly the whole trade . . . .

1805

JANUARY

6th.

Last night some young men arrived with four horses which they had stolen from the Assiniboines, (which had been stolen from them by the Assiniboines on the 18th of last month) among which was one belonging to the Company but now, by Indian law, belongs to him who risked his life in the stealing of him. They offered him to me for something less than another would have cost me. Being in want of horses I took him at the following price: 1 blanket, 1 *casse-tête à calumet*, 100 balls and powder, 1 pair leggings, 1 lance, 1 knife, 1 hoe, 1 eyed dag, a few beads.

The White Wolf, my landlord, also purchased two of his own horses back again from the same young men . . . .

. . . .

There has been no trade going on this long while, but it is impossible to refrain making some small daily expenses, which, though they appear nothing or next to nothing, run away with more goods than is expected. Thinking on this to-day and being anxious to know how I stood in my accounts, desired Mr. McKenzie to take a general inventory of his returns and remaining goods, intending to do so myself to-morrow, as the tending of the horses prevented my doing so to-day. Captain Clarke upon being informed that I had to take care of the horses myself, and they they were in danger of being thieved, desired I would send them down, and that he would have them taken care of with his own. [10]

My landlord went down to the Americans to get his gun mended; they have a very expert smith who is always employed

[9] The French measure, then in use in the North-West, *une brasse,* 5.3 English feet. *Stroud* is a coarse blanket.

[10] C. Mac Kenzie: "Wm. La Rocque and I having nothing very particular claiming attention, we lived contentedly and became intimate with the gentlemen of the American expedition, who on all occasions seemed happy to see us, and always treated us with civilty and kindness."

Francois Larocque

making different things and working for the Indians, who are grown very fond of them, although they disliked them at first . . . .

. . . .

30th.

Went down to the American Fort to get my compass put in order, the glass being broken and the needle not pointing due north, and to see how the horses were. Arrived there at 2 P.M. Fine weather.

Territorial claims of the U.S.

The Captains are busy making charts of the country through which they had passed, and delineating the Head of the Missouri according to the information they had from the Indians, who described a river as being four days march west of the last navigable part of the Missouri, which river, they say, is very large; and the Natives — whom they call "Snake Indians" or "Flat Heads" — who inhabit thereabout go, in a certain season of the year, to that river and live there entirely on fish. The course of that river, they say, is nearly south and has a placid current. The Captains make no doubt but that is a south branch of the Columbia or Ouragan River; I think it is the route they will take.

Having nothing to do at the lodge, I remained here a couple of days, being pressed to do so by the Captains. They took observations of the longitude and latitude of the place while I was with them and often since their arrival here.

They differ much from Mr. Thompson in the longitude of this place and say that Mr. Thompson has placed these villages and this part of the river a great deal too westerly, which they think is the case with all his observations for the longitude. They observed, sometime ago, an eclipse of the Moon, which, they say, is an infallible rule for finding the exact longitude of a place. But they do not differ from him in the latitude.

They include in their territory as for north as River *Qui appelle*, for, as it was impossible for a line drawn west from the west end of *Lac des Bois* to strike the Mississippi, they make it run till it strikes its tributary waters, that is, the north branches of the Missouri and from thence to the Pacific, which could not have been done while Louisiana belonged to the French or Spanish, as those Powers would not have suffered England to give a country that did not belong to it, and, of course, a line drawn west would have stopped when it struck Spanish or French territory. Capt. Lewis fixed my compass very well, which took him a whole day.[11]

. . . .

FEB.
6th. Preparing myself in snow shoes, &c., for going to the Fort, despairing of the people's coming this winter, and being in absolute want of goods, not for these Indians, for the rascals do nothing, but for Assiniboines who are upon this river and, to all appearances, loaded with furs, and who are going to the Fort only in the Spring.

7th.
The Re-
turn. Took an inventory of my remaining goods amounting to 45½ plues, and delivered them to Mr. McKenzie. Bought a dog to carry our provisions on the voyage and paid him 20 rounds of ammunition, 1 knife, 1 awl, 13 china beads and a little vermillon. Set off with Morrison at sunset; walked five hours, and encamped in the plains.

. . . .

Set off at half after six; course, north 2½ hours, when we stopped on a hill from whence we could see two large ranges of hills between which we had passed, one bearing S.E. and the other S.W.; River *La Souris* right before us, north; a large hill, called "The Black hill" lying west of north of us. Crossed River *La Souris* at half after nine and proceeded due north; leaving the Black Hill to our right; camped at 5 o'clock in the plains without wood; we made some water with snow in a tin kettle on a fire of buffalo dung which we had trouble enough in gathering, the ground being covered with nine inches of snow.

Slept till 10 o'clock, but the wind and cold would not allow us to remain any longer, so we set off and walked till half past two in the morning when we laid down in a hollow to wait for day break, the moon being set and the weather cloudy.

10th.
Severe
cold. Rose at day break and found ourselves buried in snow, it snowing very hard and blowing from the north west most violently,

[11] C. Mac Kenzie: "The woman, who answered the purpose of wife to Charbonneau, was of the Serpent nation and lately taken a prisoner by a war party. She understood a little *Gros Ventres*, in which she had to converse with her husband, who was a Canadian and did not understand English. A mulatto, who spoke bad French and worse English, served as interpreter to the Captains, so that a single word to be understood by the party required to pass from the Natives to the women, from the women to the husband, from the husband to the mulatto, from the mulatto to the captains."

so that we could not see ten steps before us, on account of drifting snow. I froze the end of my finger, in belting my blanket round me in the morning. Luckily we had not untackled our dog over night, so that we were soon ready.

Walked as hard as we could all day, but the strength of the wind greatly impeded our progress and made us go about six miles east of our course, which was north. Crossed the deep ravine at 10 A.M., its course is south east. At sunset, despairing of finding the wood before dark on the course we were going, and the bad weather continuing, we struck for River *La Souris*, north by east, at which river we arrived at half past seven. There being no wood upon that part of the river, we again slept without fire, but found a great quantity of reeds and bulrushes in which we buried ourselves, and passed the night. Bad weather continues.

Set off at 6 A.M., following the south side of the river, but at some distance; — our course north; — arrived at the woods at 10 A.M., being the Elk Head, where we stopped to dry our shoes and refresh ourselves with a few ears of roasted corn, which was all the provisions we had. The weather clearing up, we set off at 3 P.M., course north, the river running nearly the same course; — crossed the river and encamped in some Indian encampments. 11th.

Set off at 3 A.M., following an Indian road which led to the Fort; — course west of north all day; River *La Souris* running parallel with us for about 1½ miles, when it gradually turned to the east. Crossed *Rivière aux Prunes* at 4 P.M.; passed my wintering house of last year at 6, and arrived at Fort Assiniboine at 8 P.M. Mr. Chaboillez was absent, having gone to River Pain Binat. Heard the news of the death of Simon McTavish, Esq., and the joining of the two companies.[12] 12th.

. . . .

[12] Mr. Larocque remained only a few days at Fort Assinboine, then returned to the Missouri with the intention of extending his trading venture further to the west; see, "The Mississouri Indians", by Charles Mac Kenzie.

François Larocque

JOURNAL OF LAROCQUE.

INTRODUCTION.

In a letter dated November 7th, 1806, Sir Alexander Mackenzie writes his cousin, Roderick McKenzie, of the North West Company: 'When I wrote you respecting the publication of the second edition of my voyages, I had not the most distant idea that it was the intention of the Company to give the History of the Northwest, and now, instead of asking your assistance, I offer you mine, as you are the person that seems to take the lead.' In a foot-note to this letter, in his *Bourgeois de la Compagnie du Nord-Ouest*, L.R. Masson throws some further light upon this project: "The Hon. R. McKenzie was a man of considerable literery attainments and very extensive reading. He appears to have at one time entertained the idea of publishing a History of the Aboriginal tribes of the Northwest, as well as a History of the Northwest Company. In order to procure the necessary materials for that work, he sent printed circulars to many of the wintering partners and clerks of the Northwest Company, requesting them to collect, and send to him in the form of letters or journals, such information as they could obtain relating to the country in which they were respectively stationed; the natives, their origin, religion, morals and customs; their most eminent chiefs, their government; the origin of their trade with the white, &c. He received in response several reports, "accounts," and journals from the Northwest,—some of which are published in this collection *(Bourgeois de la Compagnie du Nord-Ouest)*—but he does not appear to have carried out his original plan, but seems to have been content with collecting a vast number of most interesting extracts from the books of different travellers and writers, and arranging them so as to prove and establish a perfect analogy of race between the Aborigines of the Northwest and other nations, ancient and modern, throughout the world, by the similarity of their ideas, customs and modes of living."

The material so gathered by Roderick McKenzie, or most of it, came eventually into the hands of Senator Masson, and a selection of it was published, with an introduction and notes, in his *Bourgeois de la Compagnie du Nord-Ouest*. After the death of Senator Masson these valuable documents were sold at auction, many being acquired by the

Dominion Archives, other by the Library of McGill University. Among those in the McGill Library is a draft outline of Roderick McKenzie's projected work, which apparently was to have been in two volumes. It is entitled: 'Some Account of the Northwest Company. Containing Analogy of Nations Ancient and Modern. By Roderick Mackenzie, Esq., a Director Member of the Legislative Council of Lower Canada, Lieut.-Col. of Militia, Member of the Literary and Historical Society of Quebec, Member of the American Antiquarian Society, and Fellow of the Royal Society; of Northern Antiquities at Copenhagen.' Whether Roderick McKenzie was appalled at the magnitude of the task he had undertaken, or discouraged by its cost, there is no means of knowing; at any rate his ambitious work never saw the light, in spite of its elaborate title-page.

Among the journals that McKenzie had obtained for his work were the narratives of a series of expeditions overland from the Assiniboine to the Mandan villages on the Missouri. These journals, by François Antoine Larocque, and Charles Mackenzie, clerks in the employ of the Northwest Company, covered the years 1804, 1805 and 1806, and are interesting, not only because of the light they throw upon the history of the fur trade, but also on account of the particulars they furnish as to the life and customs of one of the most remarkable of western tribes, the Mandans. Larocque's 'Missouri Journal, 1804-05,' and the first part of Charles Mackenzie's 'Mississouri Indians,' cover the same journey. The expedition was in charge of Laroque, and Mackenzie accompanied him as an assistant.

In the second expedition, of a much more ambitious nature than the first, Laroque was again in charge, with Mackenzie as assistant. Of this journey, or a portion of it, an account is given in Mackenzie's 'Second Expedition, 1805,' but until quite recently Larocque's own narrative has not been available. It may have formed part of the material collected by Roderick McKenzie, but if so was not acquired by Masson, and in fact does not seem to have been known to him. References are made in Mackenzie's narrative of his 'Third Expedition, 1805,' to Larocque's journal, but for a long time no trace could be found of the document itself. In fact the original journal is still missing, but what purports to be an exact copy is now in the Library of Laval University, Montreal, with a number of other manuscripts bequeathed to that institution by the late Judge Baby of Montreal. This 'Journal of a Voyage to the Rocky Mountains from my leaving the Assinibois River on the 2nd June, 1805,' as it is entitled, is now printed for the first time, being, so far as can be ascertained at present, a verbatim transcript of the original.

Mackenzie accompanied Larocque only as far as the Mandan and Minnetaree villages on the Missouri. Up to that point each journal forms an admirable commentary upon the other, as in the case of the previous expedition. Mackenzie also supplements Larocque in regard to the preparations for the latter's journey from the Missouri villages to the country of the Rocky Mountain Indians, or Crows, and the attempts of some of the Minnetarees to block the enterprise. From the time of Larocque's final departure, however, until his return in October, nothing has hitherto been known of his movements beyond Mackenzie's meagre reference, in his 'Third Expedition.' 'On the 18th November,' he says (he was a month out, Larocque's journal proving that he returned on the 18th October), 'to our great joy our worthy friend Mr. Larocque and his party made their appearance from their visit to the Rocky Mountain. It is not necessary that I should give the particulars of his journey, as Mr. Larocque himself has kept an account of it, I shall merely observe that he was disappointed in his expedition, suffered great hardships and took no less than thirty-six days on his return to our establishment.' It was thirty-four days, to be strictly accurate.

Before going further it may be worth while to quote an interesting passage from Daniel Williams Harmon's 'Journal of Voyages and Travels in the Interior of North America.' Under date of April 10th, 1805, he writes:

'While at Montagne à la Basse, Mr. Chaboillez induced me to consent to undertake a long and arduous tour of discovery. I am to leave that place, about the beginning of June, accompanied by six or seven Canadians, and by two or three Indians. The first place at which we shall stop will be the Mandan Village, on the Missouri River. Thence, we shall steer our course towards the Rocky Mountain, accompanied by a number of the Mandan Indians, who proceed in that direction every spring, to meet and trade with another tribe of Indians, who reside on the other side of the Rocky Mountain. It is expected that we shall return from our excursion in the month of November next.'

To this statement Harmon added the following, apparently when preparing his narrative for publication: 'This journey I never undertook; for soon after the plan of it was settled, my health became so much impaired, that I was under the necessity of proceeding to Headquarters, to procure medical assistance. A Mr. La Rocque attempted to make this tour, but went no farther than the Mandan Village.' This last statement reveals remarkable ignorance of the extent of Laroque's journey; all the more strange when it is remembered that Harmon and Larocque were members of the same fur company and that Harmon was upon terms of intimacy with Charles J.B. Chaboillez, the *Bourgeois* or partner in charge of the Upper Red River, or Assiniboine, Department, who had sent Larocque upon his journey, and to whom he reported upon his return. Possibly, from motives of trade policy or for some other reason, the particulars of Larocque's journey may have been so carefully suppressed at the time, that even Harmon was ignorant as to its extent. It will be clear, also, after reading Larocque's narrative, that Harmon was inaccurate as to the movements of the Indians, upon whom he relied to accompany him to the 'Rocky Mountain.'

The special interest of Larocque's journal lies in the fact that it describes the first visit of white men to the country of the Crow Indians, with the exception of La Vérendrye's expedition of 1742-43, and contains the earliest authoritative account of that tribe. The narrative is remarkably clear and full, bespeaking an exceptionally intelligent and wide-awake traveller; and, despite the comparatively limited field it covers, deserves to rank with such classics of the fur trade as the journals of Alexander Henry, *the Elder*, and his nephew of the same name, Daniel Williams Harmon, John McDonald of Garth, Alexander Ross, Gabriel Franchère, Charles Mackenzie and Ross Cox. Larocque's journal is in fact more readable than many more ambitious narratives of the fur trade. It contains here and there vivid touches that carry the reader back into the heart of that vanished period in western history when men of fearless, and often heroic, mould blazed new trails through a vast wilderness, taking most of the time gamblers' chances of winning through, descending unknown rivers in their frail canoes, dashing overland in midwinter from one remote trading post to another, accepting even chances of death by starvation or exposure as part of the day's work, penetrating single-handed into the territory of hostile tribes. These rough fur-traders were no saints, but nevertheless they were for the most part men of whom any country might be proud. Their faults as well as their virtues were those of a virile race. They were the true pioneers in that land of marvellous possibilities to

Francois Larocque

which all eyes are now turned, and it is not too much to say that they were largely instrumental in winning the western half of the continent to civilization.

While Larocque's narrative is chiefly notable for its descriptions of the Crows and their country, it also throws new light upon the characteristics of the Mandans and Minnetarees, and offers a valuable commentary upon the narrative of Lewis and Clark as regards those tribes of the Pacific slope, the Flatheads and Snakes. Like Alexander Henry, *the Younger*, and other chroniclers of the fur-trade period, Larocque is entirely frank as to the seamy side of native life. As Dr. Coues said of Henry's Indians, these 'are the genuine aboriginal articles, not the mock heroes of Leatherstocking romance.' For this very reason the narrative is all the more valuable as a contribution to North American ethnology.

Of the writer of this journal, François Antoine Larocque, not much is known. According to Masson, he was a brother of Joseph Larocque, who 'occupied for many years a very prominent position in the Northwest and Hudson Bay Companies.' 'Mr. F.A. Larocque,' continues Masson, 'was a man of good abilities, of great courage and energy. He was well read, studious, and equally proficient in the use of the French and English languages, but he decidedly preferred the latter. The life of an Indian trader had not for him the attractions it had for his brother; he soon left the Northwest, came to Montreal and entered business, in which he was most unfortunate. He passed the last years of his life in close retirement and arduous study, and died, much advanced in years, in the Grey nunnery of St. Hyacinthe. Mr. Larocque married a Miss Coté, the daughter of an independent Northwest trader, and the sister of Mr. Jules Maurice Quesnel. He left only one son, Mr. Alfred Larocque, the father of Mr. le Chevalier Larocque, ex-papal zouave; of Mr. Armand Larocque and of Mrs. Aldéric Ouimet, the wife of the [former] Speaker of the House of Commons.' Dr. Elliott Coues has a biographical note on Larocque, taken for the most part from Masson, in his 'Henry-Thompson Journals' (I. 361); and Joseph Tassé has a few words to say of him in his 'Canadiens de l'Ouest' (II. 324-5). Laroque is frequently mentioned in the journals of Lewis and Clark, who met him at the Mandan villages on the Missouri; and is also referred to by Alexander Henry, *the Younger*, Charles Mackenzie, and Daniel Williams Harmon.

The Journal of

Larocque's own narrative, here published, supplies some meagre details not hitherto available as to his life in the west previous to his first expedition to the Missouri with Charles Mackenzie, in the autumn of 1804. From these fragmentary notes, which will be found at the end of his journal, it appears that he left Montreal, or Lachine, on the 26th April, 1801, in the service of the X Y Company, and arrived at Grand Portage the latter end of June. From there he was sent to Fort Charlotte, on Pigeon River, and later in the year to English River, where he spent the winter. In the spring he journeyed farther west, to Fort des Prairies, on the Saskatchewan, and around to Red River. In 1802 he was still in the service of the X Y Company, but does not say where he was stationed. For the two following years he gives no particulars whatever, but we know that he was stationed at Fort Assiniboine in the autumn of 1804, and, as already stated, left with Charles Mackenzie, J.B. Lafrance, and four voyageurs, on a trip to the Mandans. His name is mentioned, as a *commis*, or clerk, in the department of *Haut de la Rivière Rouge*, in the 'Liste des bourgeois, commis, engagés, et voyageurs de la Compagnie du Nord-Ouest, apres la fusion de 1804,' at the end of v. I of Masson's *Bourgeois de la Compagnie du Nord-Ouest*.

The accompanying map will be of assistance in following Larocque step by step, from his departure from Fort a la Bosse, on the Assiniboine, on June 2nd, 1805, to his return to the same place on October 18th of the same year.

The following bibliographical notes will also be of service to those who may wish to dig deeper into the rich mines of ethnology, history and crude human nature to be found in the literature of the western fur trade. These notes serve the more immediate purpose of a commentary upon Larocque's narrative:

Larocque's personal history:

> L.R. Masson. 'Bourgeois de la Compagnie du Nord-Ouest,' I, 81 *et seq*, 299.
>
> Joseph Tassé. 'Les Canadiens de l'Ouest,' II, 324-5.
>
> Elliott Coues. 'Manuscript Journals of Alexander Henry and David Thompson.' I 301.
>
> Daniel Williams Harmon. 'Journal of Voyages and Travels in the Interior of North America,' Oct. 4, 1804.

Francois Larocque

North West Company:
  L.R. Masson. 'Bourgeois de la Compagnie du Nord-Ouest.'
  George Bryce. 'Remarkable History of the Hudson's Bay Company, including that of the French Traders of Northwestern Canada and of the Northwest, X Y and Astor Fur Companies.'
  'Origin and Progress of the North West Company of Canada,' London, 1811.
  'History of the Fur-Trade,' in Alexander Mackenzie's 'Voyages from Montreal to the Frozen and Pacific Oceans.'
  'Report on Canadian Archives, 1888, *Note E*, Northwest Trade.
  Report on Canadian Archives, 1890, *Note C*, Northwestern Explorations.
  Northwest manuscripts, in Canadian Archives.
  Masson papers, in McGill University Library.
  Alexander Henry. 'Travels and Adventures in Canada and the Indian Territories, 1760-1776.' Ed. by James Bain.
  Elliott Coues. 'Manuscript Journals of Alexander Henry and David Thompson.'
  Daniel Williams Harmon. 'Journal of Voyages and Travels in the Interior of North America.'
  Alexander Ross. 'Fur-Hunters of the Far West.'
  Alexander Ross. 'Red River Settlement,' London, 1856.
  Ross Cox. 'Adventures on the Columbia.'
  Gabriel Franchère. 'Narrative of a Voyage to the Northwest Coast of America.'
  Edouard Umfreville. 'The Present State of Hudson Bay.'
  H.H. Bancroft. 'History of the Northwest Coast.'
  Joseph Tassé. 'Les Canadiens de l'Ouest.'
  G. Dugas. L'ouest Canadien.
  Alexander Begg. 'History of the Northwest.'

The Mandans and other Tribes of the Upper Missouri:
  Journal of La Vérendrye, 1738-39. 'Report on Canadian Archives, 1889,' *Note A*.
  Journal of La Vérendrye, 1742-43. Canadian Archives MSS.
  Maximilian, Prince of Wied. 'Travels in the Interior of North America, 1832-34.'

The Journal of

Lewis and Clark. 'Expedition to the Sources of the Missouri,' &c., 1804-5-6.

George Catlin. 'Letters and Notes on the Manners, Customs and Condition of the North American Indians.'

George Catlin. 'O-Kee-Pa and Other Customs of the Mandans.'

Charles Mackenzie. 'The Mississouri Indians.' *In* Masson. I.

F.A. Larocque. 'The Missouri Journal, 1804-5.' *In* Masson, I.

David Thompson. Mandan tour. In his MSS. Journals, Book 9 vol. 5, Crown Lands Department, Toronto. *See* also Dr. Coues' note, in Henry-Thompson Journals, I, 301.

Alexander Henry. The Mandan Tour, 1806. 'Henry-Thompson Journals,' chap. IX.

H.R. Schoolcraft. 'Information respecting the History, Condition and Prospects of the Indian Tribes of the United States,' &c., pt. III, pp. 247 *et seq*.

Lewis H. Morgan. 'Systems of Consanguinity and Affinity of the Human Family,' 181 *et seq*.

Lewis H. Morgan. 'Houses and House Life of the American Aborigines.'

Lewis H. Morgan. 'Ancient Society.'

J.O. Dorsey. 'Study of Siouan Cults.'

J.O. Dorsey. 'Siouan Ethnology.'

The Crow Indians:

Morgan. 'Ancient Society.'

Morgan. 'Systems of Consanguinity,' &c.

J.P. Beckwourth. 'Life and Adventures.'

F.V. Hayden. 'Contributions to the Ethnography and Philology of the Indian Tribes of the Missouri Valley.'

Maximilian. 'Travels in the Interior of North America.'

Thomas Say. Vocabulary of the Uparoka or Crow. In E. James' 'Account of an Expedition,' &c.

R.G. Latham. 'Miscellaneous Contributions to the Ethnography of North America.'

M.I. Carrington. 'Ab-Sa-Ra-Ka.'

Elliott Coues. 'Henry-Thompson Journals.'

Catlin. 'North American Indians.'

Francois Larocque

The Flathead Indians:
> Lewis and Clark Expedition.
> Elliot Coues. 'Henry-Thompson Journals.'
> Gabriel Franchère. 'Narrative of a Voyage,' &c.
> Paul Kane. 'Wanderings of an Artist among the Indians of North America.'
> Patrick Gass's Journal.

The Snake or Shoshone Indians:
> Lewis and Clark Expedition.
> Coues. 'Henry-Thompson Journals.'
> Maximilian. 'Travels in the Interior of North America.'

A general reference may be made, in connection with all these tribes, their manners, customs, language, habitat, &c. to that unrivalled storehouse of information, the Annual Reports of the Bureau of Ethnology of the United States.

It may be noted here that all references in foot-notes to Maximilian are to the edition included in R.G. Thwaites' 'Early Western Travels;' to Lewis & Clark, the J.K. Hosmer edition; to Gabriel Franchère's Narrative, J.V. Huntington's translation, 1854, except where otherwise specified; and to Harmon, the 1903 reprint. References to Lewis & Clark in the Bibliographical notes are understood to include also the Coues' and Thwaites' editions. The exhaustive notes added to these editions increase enormously the value of the work, from the historical, ethnographical, geographical and scientific points of view.

François Larocque

JOURNAL OF A VOYAGE TO THE ROCKY MOUNTAINS FROM MY LEAVING THE ASSINIBOIS[1] RIVER ON THE 2nd JUNE, 1805.

At my arrival at Rivière Fort de la Bosse[2] I prepared for going on a voyage of discovery to the Rocky Mountains and set off on the 2nd June with two men having each of us two horses, one of which was laden with goods to facilitate an intercourse with the Indians we might happen to see on our road. Mr. Charles McKenzie[3] and Mr. Lassana[4] set out with me to go & pass the summer at the Missouri, and having to parsue the same road we Kept Company as far as the B.B.[5] village.

Mr. McKenzie with the other men set of about at two in the afternoon, but I having [been] so very busy that I had not as yet been able to write my letters to my friends remained and wrote letters and settled some little business of my own. After sunset we supped & bidding farewell to Mr. Chabelly[6] & Henry[7] & to all the people, departed, every one being

[1] One of the innumerable variants of the name Assiniboine. This main branch of the Red River has also borne various other names, the first of which was Rivière St. Charles, given by La Vérendrye, the first white man to stand upon its banks. In the manuscript map of David Thompson, astronomer of the Northwest Company, it is called Stone Indian River. See footnote, p. 45, Coues' 'Henry-Thompson Journals.'

[2] Larocque elsewhere calls this trading post Mount a la Bosse.

[3] McKenzie joined the Northwest Company in 1803 as an apprentice clerk, made an expedition to the Mandan villages on the Missouri in 1804, in which he was accompanied by Larocque, and, as above stated, again travelled with Larocque in 1805 as far as the Missouri. He made a third journey to the Mandans in the fall of the same year, and a fourth in 1806. His narratives of the four journeys are printed in Masson, V.I. See Masson's biographical note, p. 317, and Coues', p. 345.

[4] No such name in Roderick McKenzie's list of 'Proprietors, clerks, interpreters, &c., of the Northwest Company, 1799,' nor in the 'Liste des bourgeois, commis, engages, et voyageurs de la Compagnie du Nord-Ouest, après la fusion de 1804,' Masson, I, 395. May be intended for J.B. Lafrance, mentioned by Charles McKenzie as of the party.

[5] Big Bellies, called by the French, Gros Ventres. The name has been applied at different times and by different writers to two quite distinct tribes: the Atsina (called Fall Indians by Umfreville, and Rapid Indians, by Alexander Henry), and the Minnetarees or Hidatsas. The former are of Algonquian, and latter of Siouan, stock.

[6] Charles Jean-Baptiste Chaboillez, 'Bourgeois' or partner of the Northwest Company, at this time in charge of the Assiniboine department. See Masson, I, 81, and footnote; also Coues, p. 60, note.

[7] Alexander Henry, known as *the Younger* to distinguish him from his uncle, Alexander Henry, *the Elder*, whose 'Travels and Adventures in Canada and the Indian Territories' was first published in 1809 (new ed. by Dr. James Bain, 1901.) The voluminous manuscript journals of Henry *the Younger* were edited by Dr. Elliott Coues, in conjunction with those of David Thompson, under the title, 'New Light on the Early History of the Greater Northwest,' New York, 1897. Chap. IX contains Henry's account of the Mandan Tour, 1806.

[8] Pipestone river, or creek, a branch of the Souris river coming in from the west. I cannot find the name given by Larocque in this locality on any of the maps.

affected at our departure thinking it more than probable that I should not return with my men, and I confess I left the fort with a heavy heart but riding at a good rate I soon got chearful again, and thought of nothing but the [means] of ensuring success to my undertaking.

At 10 at night I arrived at the River aux Prunes[8] where I found the people encamped asleep.

Monday 3rd. I sat of early in the morning and stopped at 12 to refresh our horses, and encamped at night at River la Sorie,[9] where we had not been two hours encamped when three, and after many other Assiniboins rushed in upon us, a few endeavouring to take our horses, but seeing our guns and running to them we made them depart. They ran afterwards to our fire and seeing us well armed and by our looks that we would well defend ourselves and our property they remained quiet. There were 40 tents of them not 10 acres from us without that we had perceived them. I gave 1 fm. tobacco[10] to their Chief to make his young men smoke & engage them to remain peaceable. Some of them offered to accompany us to the Missouri, but upon being told that we would like it well they spoke no more of it.

Thinking it hower not prudent to pass the night so close to them we saddled our horses and departed although they did all in their power of engaging us to sleep at those tents. One of them conducted us to a good fording place of River la Sourie which we crossed striking in the plain. We walked all night to come out of their reach for they are worst cunning horse thieves that ever I said or heard of. A little before day light we stopped and took a nap.

Tuesday 4th. We proceeded on our journey early in the morning having very fine weather all day, and at night encamped on the banks of the River la Sourie at a place called Green River[11] for its having no wood on its side for about 30 miles. We saw no other animals but four cabois[12] of which we killed two.

Wednesday 5th. We followed the Green River till eleven o'clock when

[9] Elsewhere Larocque spells it River la Sourie. The Souris appears as Mouse river on some of the older maps.

[10] The Brazil tobacco, so-called, used in trade by the North West and Hudson's Bay Companies, was prepared in the torm ot a rope, and cut off as required. Larocque cut off 1 fathom as a present to placate the Assiniboines. See Dr. Bain's note, p. 321, Henry's 'Travels and Adventures.' The fathom, according to Masson, was the French measure then in use in the Northwest, *une brasse*.

[11] Cut Bank creek, rising close to the International Boundary, and joining the Souris in the sout. ern part of Bottineau county, N.D. Alexander Henry calls it Rivière Plé.

[12] Elsewhere Larocque spells it caribo. The animal referred to is the familiar American antelope, *antilocapra americana*.

Francois Larocque

we arrived at the woods, where being an appearance of rainy weather we encamped. There was no Buffalo in seight. At 12 it began to rain and continued hard and uninterruptedly until next morning. Here we saw plenty of wild fowls, Ducks, Bustards, Geese, Swans, &c., and killed a number of them.

Thursday 6th. There being an appearance of fine weather, we sat off and walked about three miles, when the weather being cloudy we stopped to encamp, but before we could make a hut for our goods the rain began again, and fell amasingly hard so that in a few hours every hollows or valley in the plains were full of water, and every brook or creek was swellen to rivers. There were plenty of Buffaloes and the rain ceasing in the evening we killed a very fat young bull[13] and a fat Elk deer. At night the rain began again and continued without intermission until morning.

Friday 7th. The weather continued cloudy, but the sun appearing now and then we hoped for fair weather and past of but as yesterday it began to rain at 12, at two we found some wood on some sandy hills in the plains where we stopped to cook our goods, being completely trenched [drenched]. There being no water on the sand hills, we raised a Bark of Elm tree and pulling one end in a Kettle, the other end a little higher, all the water that fell on the Bark ran into the kettle and we had presently a sufficient quantity; we also made a tent with bark and passed the night comfortably enough.

Saturday 8th. We sat of to go to a hill called Grosse Butte[14] to dry our things, and water our horses, but their being none here, arrived there two hours and a half where we stopped for the remainder of the day & night. The Grosse Bute is a high hill which is seen at 20 miles off on either side. At its foot on the north side is a Lake of about 8 miles in circumference in which there are middle sized pikes. Between the Lake and the hill there is some wood chiefly Elm; all around are many lakes, which by the late rain communicated with each other. From the top of the hill the turtle mountain[15] was soon being due North, River la Sourie likewise was of in

[13] 'In the early part of the season,' says Alexander Ross in his 'Red River Settlement,' 'the bulls are fat and the cows lean; but in the autumn the case is the reverse, the bulls are lean and the cows fat.'

[14] The position of this hill is sufficiently indicated in the next paragraph. Dr. Coues identifies Grosse Butte with present White Rock hill, North Dakota.

[15] Turtle Mountain is a well-known landmark, lying across the parallel of 49°, partly in Canadian and partly in United States territory. It is constantly referred to in the journals of fur-traders and explorers, the old Indian thoroughfare between the Assiniboine and the Missouri passing around it to the westward.

N.N.E. and south and south west, being seen on all sides of the hill excepted west.

Sunday 9th. We sat of early in the morning, in a course S.S.W. and at 1 o'clock in the afternoon we arrived on the Bank of the River la Sourie.[16] The water being amazing high we made a raft to cross our things over the River and the horses swam over. We saddled immediately and encamped in a Coulé[17] about three miles from the River.

Monday 10th. Leaving this we went and slept in the Mandan plain,[18] saw plenty of buffaloes all along, but did not dare to fire at them, being on the enemies lands is Sioux.[19] It rained a little in the night.

Tuesday 11th. At 8 in the morning I saw the banks of the Missoury,[20] at 12 arrived at the River Bourbeuse,[21] when we unsad[dl]ed our horses where we unloaded our horses and crossed the property on our shoulders there being not more than 2 feet of water, but we sunk up to our middle in mud, the horses bemired themselves in crossing and it was with difficulty we got them over the bank beings bogs as also the bed of the river. We intended to get the villages today but being overtaken by a Shower of rain we encamped in a coulé at the Serpent lodge,[22] being a winter village of the B. Belly's at the Elbow of the River, where I passed part of last winter. Being unwilling to untie my things before the Indians of the village as I was necessarily be put to some expence I took here a small equipment of different article for present expense, as the sight of my goods would perhaps cause the B.B. to refuse our passage to the Rocky Mountains.

Wednesday 12th. I arrived at 9 o'clock in the morning on the banks of the Missoury, fired a few shots to inform the Indians of our being there and in a few hours many came over with Canoes to cross us and our things.

---

[16] He crosses the Souris about its most southerly point, where it is nearest to the Missouri.

[17] A deep gully. This is probably one of the earliest instances of the use of the term.

[18] The Coteau du Missouri, or tableland separating the waters of the Missouri from those of the Assiniboine.

[19] All this country west of Red River and between the boundary and the Missouri was Sioux territory. The traveller, white or red, who came this way, stepped warily. It was as well not to meet these fierce and crafty warriors of the plains. When Alexander Henry ascended Red River in 1800 he had the greatest difficulty in preventing his men from turning back, when they reached the borders of the Sioux country.

[20] Charles McKenzie, and others, spell it Mississouri; Alexander Henry, Missourie. Other variants are found in narratives and journals of the period.

[21] Miry Creek of Lewis & Clark, now Snake Creek, flows S.W. into the Missouri, in McLean County.

[22] Loge de Serpent, in Henry's narrative, and still known as the Snakes Den. A bold bluff at the mouth of Snake Creek.

Francois Larocque

Lafrance proceeded to the Mandans[23] but I and my men with Mr. McKenzie crossed here at the B. Belly's & entered into dift lodges, gave my men each a small equipment of Knives Tobacco and ammunition to give the landlords.[24]

Thursday 13th. Three Assiniboins arrived in the evening. 4 Canadians from the Illinois, who are hunting Beaver in these parts, came to see me. I gave each of them 6 inches of [Brazil] Tobacco which pleased them very much as they had for several months not smoked any but Indian Tobacco.

Fryday 14th. The Indians here are exceedingly troublesome to sell their horses to us, the prise that we usually pay them for a horse can purchas two from the Rocky Mountain Indians who are expected dayly, & they would wish us to have more goods when those Indians arrive, so as to have the whole trade themselves. I told them that the purpose of our coming was not to purchase horses either from them or the Rocky Mountains, that we came for Skins and Robes and that for that purpose one of us was to pass the summer with them and one at the Mandans; that I and two men were sent by the white people's Chief[25] to smoke a pipe of peace & amity with the Rocky Mountain Indians and to accompany them to their lands to examine them and see if there were Beavers as is reported & to engage them to hunt it, that we would not purchase a horse from none, therefore that their best plan would be to dress Buffalo Robes, so as to have ammunition to trade with the Rocky Mountain Indians.

They pretend to be in fear of the surrounding nations, that is Assineboines,[26] Sioux,[27] Cheyennes[28] & Ricaras,[29] so as to have an excuse

---

[23] No American tribe, with the possible exception of the Iroquois, has excited more interest and curiosity than the Mandans. Certain peculiarities in their language, habits, and physical appearance have given rise to much speculation as to their origin. The first white man to visit the Mandans was Pierre Gaultier de Varennes, Sieur de La Vérendrye, the narrative of whose journey will be found in the Archives Report, 1889, pp. 2-29. John McDonnell records what appears to be the earliest visit of British traders to the Mandans. (Masson, I, 273.)

[24] The traders were usually guests of some leading member of the tribe, but remuneration in the form of gifts was always expected and given.

[25] In this case, the *bourgeois* Chaboillez. For the native attitude toward the 'white people's Chief' see Masson, I, 383-4.

[26] See the manuscript journals and letters of Pierre de La Vérendrye and his sons, in the Dominion Archives. See footnote, pp. 269-70, 'Contributions to the Historical Society of Montana, I (1876, 2nd ed.); Maximilian, I, 387 *et seq.* The Assiniboines were of Siouan stock.

[27] The earliest accounts of the Naudowessi or Sioux are contained in the Jesuit Relations. Other records of the same period are the Letters of Daniel Greyselon Du Lhut and Father Guignas (Dominion Archives, 'Posts in the Western Sea,' Vol. 16); and the Voyages of Pierre Esprit Radisson (Prince Society, 1885); and Pike's 'Expeditions to Headwaters of the Mississippi' (Coues' ed.), 1, 341 *et seq.*

for not trading their guns with the Rocky Mountain Indians, and likewise to prevent us. Some of those Rocky Mountain Indians have been here already and are gone back, but more are expected, with whom I intend to go.

Saturday 15th. I was sent for by one of the Chiefs who asked me what I intended to do with the pipe stem I had brought, upon my telling him that it was for the Rocky Mountain Indians he made a long harangue to dissuade me from going there, saying that I would be obliged to winter there on account of the length of the way, that the Cheyennes and Ricaras were enemies and constantly on the Road, and that it was probable we should be killed by them. He gave the worst character possible to the Rocky Mountain Indians, saying they were thieves and liar, of which he gave an example that is of a Canadian of the name of Menard,[30] who had lived here about 40 years and a few years ago sett of to go to the Rocky Mountains to trade horses and Beavers, these Indians did all in their power to prevent him, but seeing him absolutely bent upon going they let him go, he arrived at the Rocky Mountain Indians tents, where he was well treated, & got 9 horses and 2 female slaves, besides a quantity of Beaver, he left the lodge very well pleased, but were followed by some young men who in the night stole 7 horses, a few nights after his 2 Slaves deserted with the other horses and other young men coming took from him everything he had even to his knife, he came crying to the B.B. Village almost dead having but his robe to make shoes (with flint stone) which he tied about his feet with cords, which so pained the B.B. that they killed some of the Roche Mountain[31] for revenge & &. he told me many other stories, to all which I answered that my Chief had sent me to go, and that I would or die.

There is seven nights that 5 young men are gone to meet the Rocky Mountain Indians, they are expected dayly & the Rocky Mountain with them.

[28] Charles Mackenzie calls them Shawyens or Chawyens, and describes a visit to their country, in his Fourth Expedition (Masson, I, 373 *et seq*.) An earlier account of the same tribe is found in La Verendrye's 1742-44 Journal already cited. They belong to the Algonquin family.

[29] Originally Pawnees, who settled on the Missouri below the Cheyennes, and later moved down to the neighbourhood of the Mandans.

[30] Probably the same Menard who, according to Alexander Henry, 'was pillaged and murdered by three Assiniboines in 1803, on his way to the Missourie.'

[31] *i.e.*, Rocky Mountain Indians.

François Larocque

Sunday 16th. This Evening the Indian women danced the scalp of a Black feet[32] Indian which they killed the last spring. The Canadians from below said they had killed some white men at the same time, that they had seen cloths such as Corduroy Jackets and trousers, collars, shirts, part of Linnen Tents, Casimer[33] waist coats, and many other things belonging to the whites. The Borgne[34] the Great Chief of this village told me that war party had fired upon and killed people who were going down a very large River, in skin canoes,[35] but that they could not tell whether they were Crees[36] or Sauteux[37] or whites. I spoke to old Cerina Grape[38] the father of the Chief of that party, and to the Chief himself, they prove by the fire, Earth and Heaven that they were not whites. They made a plan of the Country through which they passed, and in my opinion it is some where [about] the Sas Ratchewini[39] or its branches. They showed me part of what they plundered but I saw nothing that could prove them to have killed Whites except the quantity of gun powder he had, for it was no less than half a Keg and at least 200 balls. Their plunder was parted among all the warriors and their relations. Among the articles that the Cerina Grappe showed me there was a Coat made of the skin of a young horse wrought with porcupine quills and human hair, 2 skunk skins guarnished with red stroud and blue beads which those Indians generally wear round their ancles, one musket by Ketland one gun by Barnett,[40] and lastly one scalp which was evidently that of an Indian. But I really believe they have

[32] The earliest account of the Blackfeet is contained in the Journal of Anthony Hendry (Trans., Royal Society of Canada, 1907.) See also Matthew Cocking's Journal. (Trans. Royal Society of Canada, 1908.)

[33] *i.e.*, Cashmere.

[34] This very remarkable Indian figures prominently in all contemporary Missouri narratives. See Charles Mackenzie's Mississouri Indians (Masson, I); Henry-Thompson Journals, pp. 259, 322, 346, etc.; Lewis & Clark, ch. vi and xviii.

[35] The 'bull-boat' of the Missouri and Saskatchewan, of which an excellent representation is given in one of Bodmer's plates (Maximilian's Travels.)

[36] The Crees, of Algonquian stock, covered in Larocque's day an immense territory. Under the name of Christineaux, or innumerable variants: Cristinapx, Kilistinaux, Kinistinces, Knistineaux, and so forth, this numerous tribe is constantly referred to in the Jesuit Relations and the narratives of fur-traders, explorers and travellers, down to the close of the period of French rule in Canada, and later. They were found anywhere around Lake Superior, the Red River country, Lake Winnipeg, sometimes as far west as the upper Missouri and the South Saskatchewan, and north-west even to the Peace River and the Mackenzie.

[37] Chippewas, sometimes known as Ojibways. Of Algonquian stock.

[38] Not elsewhere referred to under this name.

[39] Saskatchewan. In La Vérendrye's day it went under a different name, variously spelled, Poskoiac, Pasquayah, Basquia, etc.

[40] Well-known English makers of the period.

killed some white people about Fort Des Prairies[41] for they brought more goods than ever I saw in the possession of Indians at one time.

Monday 17th. I went down to the Mandan Village on horse back and purchased a saddle there for which I paid 30 lbs ammunition desired Lafrance to get some provision made for my voyage as there is no corn where I live.[42] I returned home to my lodge. In the evening having settled some business with a man of the name of Jusseaux[43] who was indebted to the Company.

Tuesday 18th. The son of the White Wolf fell from his horse and bruised his leg terribly, the flesh was taken clean of the bone from the ancle, round the leg to the calf. The Indian doctor was sent for who began his cure by blowing and singing while the child suffered quietly. Thunder storm.

Wednesday 19th. There being another sick person in my Lodge and there being rather too much fuss about medicines, conjuring & singing I went & lived in another lodge where I had placed one of my men before. Went to see the Borgne our Chief and being desirous that he should stand by me in case of need I made him a present of ¾ lb. Tobacco, one knife and 50 Rounds of ammunition at which he was well pleased—he is the greatest Chief in this place, but does not talk against our going to the Rocky Mountains as the other Chiefs do—Thunder and rain at night.

Thursday 20th. I was again teased by some of the Chief to purchase horses and was told the Big Bellys had two hearts[44] and that they not know whether they would allow me to go to the Rocky Mountains, and in the course of a long harangue they made use of all their art to induce me not to go representing the journey as dangerous to the last degree and that the Rocky Mountain would not come, for they were afraid of the Ricaras & Assiniboines to all which I could make no answer but by signs, as there was no one present that could speak to them properly, one of my men of the name of Souci[45] spoke the Sioux language but there was no one there that understood that language. About [noon] two of the young B.B. that had been sent to meet the Rocky Mountains arrived, they left the Rocky

[41] Several different trading posts on the Saskatchewan bore this name. The one mentioned by Larocque was on the South Saskatchewan.

[42] That is, on the Assiniboine.

[43] Mentioned by Masson as having resided in the Missouri country as an independent trader for over fifteen years, and as having served as guide and interpreter to Mr. David Thompson in his voyage of exploration of 1797.

[44] Or as we would say, were of two minds.

[45] Pierre Saucie's name is included under the department of *Haut de la Rivière Rouge*, in the *Liste des bourgeois* etc., at the end of vol. I of Masson.

Mountain Indians in the morning and they will be here in 3 or 4 days. Upon the receipt of those news, the Chief pretended to have received information that the Crils[46] & Assiniboines were assembled to come and war upon them (which is false) and harangues were made to the people to keep their guns and ammunitions and not to trade them with the Rocky Mountain Indians, &c. All this I believe a scheme to prevent me from going, for as yet they do not like to tell me so exactly, but are for ever saying that they have two hearts which means that they are undetermined in what manner to act.

Fryday 21st. I went to see the Borgne enquired of him what he and the Big Bellys thought of our going to the Rocky Mountains and whether they have a mind to prevent us. He answered to my wish, that the Rocky Mountains were good people, that they had plenty of Beaver on their hands, and that his adopted son, one of the Chiefs of the Rocky Mountains & the greater would take care of us, for that he would strongly recommend to him to put the white people in his heart and watch over them. I told him that the B.B. had no reason to be displeased for that one of us remains with them who has plenty of ammunition, Knives, tobacco, Hatchets and other articles, where with to supply their wants, whenever they would be disposed to trade. He said it was true that none would molest us.[47] He is the only Chief that speaks so, but as he has the most authority of any I hope by his means we will pass. A certain method to get the road clear would be to assemble the Chiefs, make them a present of Tobacco and ammunition, make them smoke & speak to them what occasion I may have for them in future. I like not to do it only when I see that I cannot otherwise for assembling a Council and haranging without a present is no better than speaking to a heap of stones. Besides I am apprehensive that paying as it were for our first going to these nations will give a footing to the B. Bellys which they will endeavoure to improve every time we should go there if a trading interest takes place. So we pass this time without making them any present at all, I believe it will be done away for ever. If the Borgne retains that authority he formerly had he alone will be able to clear the Road for us and he appears to be sincerely our friend.

Saturday 22nd. In the beginning I went to an Indian's tent whose two sons had been in that party that defeated the White on the Saskatchion, he gave me a full account and more like truth than any other. He says there

---

[46] Another variant of the name Crees.
[47] Charles Mackenzie's version of this speech is found in Masson I, 344.

were four Linnen tents and four leather on the sides of the River where there were Skin Canoes; they fired upon the largest leather tent and Killed three men, two of whom were Indians, the other they believe to be a White man but not certain. They brought one scalp & if it is that which they showed me, it is an Indian. There was plenty of tents in all kinds besides goods. What they could not take with them, they broke and threw in the River.

Sunday 23rd. Three men and one woman arrived from the Rocky Mountains about noon, the other are near hand and would have arrived today but for rain which fell in the evening.

In the evening I went to see the Brother of the Borgne, where I found two Rocky Mountain Indians, one of whom was the Chief of whom the Borgne had spoken with me.[48] I smoked with them for some time when the Borgne told them that I was going with them and spoke very much in our favor. They appeared to be very well pleased.

Monday 24th. Lafrance, with the other white people from below who reside at the Mandans came to see the people which were arrived from the Rocky Mountains, who were prevented from coming by appearance of bad weather. It thundered the whole day but it did not rain. I gave a small knife to my Land Lady.

Tuesday 25th. About one in the afternoon the Rocky Mountain Indians arrived, they encamped at a little distance from the village with the warriors, to the number of 645, passed through the village on horseback with their shields & other war-like implements,[49] they proceeded to the little village,[50] Souliers[51] and then to the Mandans and returned.

[48] 'Le Borgne,' says Charles Mackenzie, 'sent for us in order to introduce Mr. La Rocque to the Rocky Mountain Chief, whose name is *Nakesinia*, or Red Calf.' Masson, I, 345.

[49] Mackenzie gives a more spirited account of the arrival of the Rocky Mountain Indians. 'They consisted,' he says, 'of more than three hundred tents, and presented the handsomest sight that one could imagine; all on horseback, children of small size were lashed to the saddle and those above the age of six could manage a horse. The women had wooden saddles, most of the men had none. There were a grest many horses for the baggage and the whole, exceeding two thousand, covered a large space of ground, and had the appearance of an army. They halted on a rising ground behind the village, and, having formed a circle, the chief addressed them; they then descended full speed, rode through the village, exhibiting their dexterity in horsemanship in a thousand shapes. I was astonished to see their agility and address, and I do believe they are the best riders in the world. They were dressed in leather and looked clean and neat; some wore beads and rings as ornaments. Their arms were bows and arrows, lances and round stones enclosed in leather and slung to a shank in the form of a whip; they made use of shields, and they have a few guns.'

[50] The Minnetaree village called Metaharta by Lewis & Clark, and Awatichay by Maximilian. It was on the south side of Knife river, and was the residence of Le Borgne.

[51] The Amahami, called by the French traders Gens des Souliers, or Souliers Noirs, [Blackfeet].

Francois Larocque

There did not remain 20 persons in the village, men women and children all went to the newly arrived camp carrying a quantity of Corn raw and cooked which they traded for Leggins, Robes and dried meat. There are 20 lodges of the snake Indians[52] & about 40 men. The other bands are more numerous.

This morning the Borgne sent for me, he showed me the Rocky Mountain Chief of the Ererokas,[53] and told him before me that I was going with him & to take good care of us & he spoke very much in our favour telling me that the B. Bellys were undetermined whether they would allow us to go or not, but that we would go if we liked it for that he would clear the road before us if necessary. I gave to two of the Ererokas each 6 [feet] of tobacco and 20 Rounds of ammunitions.

Wednesday 26th. The Mandans, Souliers, little village people & the people of the Village, went on horse back and arived to perform the same ceremonys round the Rocky Mountain Camp, as the Rocky Mountains did yesterday here,[54] they were about 500, but a great many Wariors are absent being gone to war.

Thursday 27th. Assembled the chiefs of the different Bands of the Rocky Mountains and made them a present of

2 Large Axes	16 large Knives
2 Small Axes	12 Small do
8 Ivory Combs	2 lbs. Vermillion
10 Wampum Shells	8 doz. Rings
8 fire steels and Flint	4 papers co'd Glasses
4 cassetete[55]	4 Doz. Awls
6 Masses B.C. Beads[56]	1½ lb. Blue Beads
4 f. Tobacco	2 Doz. do
8 Cock feathers	1000 balls & powder

Made them smoke in a stem[57] which I told them was that of the Chief of the White people who was desirous of making them his Children &

---

[52] Shoshone Indians. They were known as the Snake Indians to Henry and other writers of the period. Their habitat was about the headwaters of the Missouri or its branches.

[53] 'The Crows,' says Granville Stuart, 'are called Absarokis, or Upsaroka.' (Contr. Hist. Soc., Montana, I, 274.)

[54] Masson, I, 345.

[55] 'B.C.' probably stands for 'Blue Canton.' John McDonnell speaks of '6 bunches blue beads,' and Larocque (in Masson) buys a dog for, among other things, '13 china beads.'

[56] In his Missouri Journal (Masson I, 309) Larocque had '1 *casse-tete a calumet*, the familiar combination of tomahawk and pipe.

[57] *i.e.*, pipe.

Brethren, that he knew they were pitiful and had no arms to defend themselves from their enemies, but that they should cease to be pityful as soon as they would make themselves brave hunters. That I and two men were going with them to see their lands and that we took with us some articles to supply their present want. That our Chief sent them those goods that lay before them, to make them listen to what we were now telling them, that he expected they would treat all white people as their Brethren for that we were in peace and friendship with the Red skined people and did not go about to get a scalp, that probably they would see White people on their lands from another quarter but that they were our brethren and of course we expected they would not hurt them, that a few years ago they pillaged and ill treated a white man who went to trade with them,[58] that we would see how they would treat us and if they have behaved well towards us and kill Beavers, Otters & Bears they would have white people on the lands in a few years, who would winter with them and supply them with all their wants & &. I told them many other things which I thought was necessary and closed the Harangue by making them smoke the Medicin Pipe.[59] They thanked [me] and make a present of 6 robes, one Tyger skin,[60] 4 shirts, 2 women Cotillons,[61] 2 dressed Elk skins, 3 saddles and 13 pair leggins. I clothed the Chief of the Ererokas at the same time[62] and gave him a flag and a Wanpoon Belt and told them that our Chief did not expect that we would pass many different nations and therefore had sent but one Chief Clothing, but that in the course of the summer we would fix upon a spot most convenient for them all where we would build & trade with them, if we saw that they wished to encourage the white people to go on their lands by being good hunters and that then all their Chiefs who would behave well would get a Coat.

The ceremony of adopting Children was going on at the same time, but I was so very busy that I could not attend, but about the middle of the ceremony, and therefore can give but an imperfect account of it from my own observation, but as the two people were present I will give an account of it in another place.

[58] The unfortunate Menard, before mentioned.

[59] Throughout all the tribes the medicine pipe was held in high veneration, and the smoking of this pipe formed an important feature of all treaties or meetings with other Indians or Whites.

[60] The puma (*Felis concolor*), also known as the panther or mountain lion, or the wildcat (*Lynx rufus fasciatus.*)

[61] Petticoats. One cotillon was valued at 7 beaver skins. See Roderick McKenzie's Reminiscences. (Masson, I, 14; also I, 87.)

[62] The presentation of a Chief's Clothing formed an important part of a visit to or from a new tribe. What the clothing consisted of may be gathered from James McKenzie's Journal (Masson, II, 384.)

Francois Larocque

Fryday 28th. I preferred to go of in the evening to the lodge of the Ereroka Chief in order to be ready with them in the morning but he and the other Chiefs were called to a farewell Council in the Borgnes Lodge so that I did not Stir.

Saturday 29th. Saddled our horses and left the B. Belly village. We remained about half an hour in the Rocky Mountain Camp where they threw down their tents and all sat of. We marched along the Knife River[63] for about eight miles when we stopped and encamped. The Borgne and many other B. Belly's came and slept with us.

Sunday 30th. We followed a south course for about 4 mile and stoped to dine and resumed a S.S.W. course and encamped for night, Knife River in Sight when no hills intervened, about 6 miles on our right, a thunder storm in the evening.

July 1st, Monday. We sat [out] at 8 o'clock in the morning and encamped at 12 having followed a South West course; we crossed three small creeks running North and N. East into the Knife River. It began to rain as soon as the lodges were pitched and continued so all day. The Indians hunted and Killed a few Bulls. I gave the people of my lodge a few articles, as Beads, Knives.

Tuesday 2nd. We sat out at 9 o'clock followed a south Course and encamped at 2 after noon. It thundered very much the whole of the afternoon and at sun set there fell such a shower of hail as I never saw before, some of the hail stones being as large as hen eggs and the rest as a Yolk; they fell with amazing violence and broke down several tents. The wind during the storm was West, it breesed to the North and continued during the whole night.

Wednesday 3rd. We continued our journey for about 4 hours, through a very hilly country and encamped at the foot of a very high Hill on the top of which I ascended, but could see at no considerable distance, another range of hills surrounding this on all sides. I lost my spy glass in coming down the hill and could not find it again. Our course was south.

Thursday 4th. We stopped after a south course for the night on the side of a small hill at a Creek[64] which empties in the Missouri above the Panis[65] village about 5 leagues distant from our last encampment having

[63] Knife River enters the Missouri from the south about long. 101° 20' W. The village from which Larocque and his friends the Crows have just departed was on the S. side of Knife River, about half a mile above its mouth. The party are therefore marching along the north bank of the river.

[64] Heart river, which empties into the Missouri a little to the east of long. 101°.

[65] Pawnees. For history and description of this tribe see Henry, I, 334; Lewis and Clark (Hosmer ed.), I, 35-36; Coues' 'Pike,' II, 532 *et seq*; Catlin, II, 27.

crossed another a little before emptying in the Missury about one mile below the Mandans. The Scouts reported that Buffaloes were at hand.

Fryday 5th. We discovered a thief last night in the act of stealing a gun from under our loads thinking we were asleep. The Chief sent two young men to sleep behind the lodge and guard our property. After three hours and a half march in a southerly direction we espied Buffaloes, and stopped all. The Chief harangued and the young men set out to hunt after which we marched on for about a league and a half and encamped. There was no Creek or River here for water only a few ponds of stagnant water which by reason of so many dogs and horses bathing in them was not drinkeable being as thick as mud.

Saturday 6th. A Big Belly found my spy glass and returned it to me, we set of at 8. At 11 the scouts reported that they had seen enemies. We all stopped, the men armed themselves and mounting their fleetest horses went in pursuit. They returned in a few hours, as what the scouts had taken for enemies were a party of their own people who were gone hunting and not been seen. We proceeded and encamped at one on the side of a small River running West and emptying in the lasser Missouri.[66] It blew a hurricane in the evening. Course south about four leagues.

Sunday 7th. At ten o'clock we rose the Camp and at 3 we saw Buffaloes, harangues were made to the Young Men to go and hunt while a party of these latter who are a guard of soldiers[67] paraded before the body of the people preventing any one from setting off till all the huntsmen were gone; after which we set off again and encamped at the foot of a hill, which we had in sight since the day before yesterday. Course S. West about 18 miles.

Monday 8th. Before we rose the camp a general muster of all the guns in the Camp was taken and the number found to be 204 exclusive of ours. Our huntsmen had brought in a plenty of Buffaloes. We marched this day by a south Course about 7 miles.

Tuesday 9th. From the Big Belly village to the place I lost my spy glass the country was very hilly, from that to this place it was much more upon a level though not entirely so. The plains produce plenty of fine

---

[66] Lesser Missouri, or Little Missouri, as it is more generally known; joins Missouri long. 102° 15'.

[67] Most of the migratory prairie tribes subjected themselves to some form of discipline on the march as well as in their temporary camps, and appointed a species of police to keep order. See La Vérendrye (Journal, Archives, 1889), and Henry *the Elder* (Bain's ed., 294) as to the Assiniboines; Hendry's Journal (R.S.C., 1907) as to the Blackfeet; Maximilian describes similar soldiers or police among the Mandans.

grass. In the course of this days journey we passed between two big hills on the top of which as far as the eye could discern Buffalo were seen in amazing number, we camped on the side of a small Creek running West into the lesser Missouri. The Indian hunted and killed many Buffaloes. Course South S. West & S.W. 9 miles. It blew a hurricane at night without rain. Many lodges were thrown down although well tied and picketted.

Wednesday 10th. We remained the greatest part of the day at this place to dry the meat and bury a woman that died here, and sat of at 4 in the afternoon and pitched the tents by a small creek running west after having pursued our road S.W. by West for 5 miles. The Country was hilly but produsing plenty of grass and numberless flowers of different Kinds.[68]

Thursday 11th. We passed through a range of hills of about 3 miles broad, on the top of every one was a heap of stones appearing as if burnt, part of the rocks had fallen down the hills. Leaving those hills we had a pretty level plain till we reach a small brook running N. West where we encamped, the lesser Missouri in Sight at about 4 miles on our right, by a course south west, we had advanced about 12 miles. On our way we saw a few Rattle Snakes but none of them very large; they are the first I saw in the Indian countries and none are to be found more northwards.

Fryday 12th. This day we passed through a pleasant plain and pitched the tents by a small brook 5 miles S.W. of our last encampment.

Saturday 13th. We set of at 9 through hilly and barren Country, in crossing two small Creeks, and arrived at 12 on the bank of lesser Missouri. We crossed it and encamped on its border about 2 miles higher. The River is here about ¾ of an acre in breadth from bank to bank but there is very little water running, the bed appearing dry in many places and is of sand and gravel. A few liards[69] scattered thinly along its banks. The rugged and barren aspect of the hills which are composed of Whitish Clay looking like rocks at a distance. The ground on which [we] stood [was covered] with a prickly heap of.....[70] so very thick that one does not know where to set ones feet, no grass at all. The whole forms a prospect far from pleasing. Our Course was for 12 miles S.S.W. A few days ago a child being sick I gave him a few drops of Turlington balsam[71] which eased him immediately of his cholic. This cure gave me such a reputation of being a

---

[68] See Maximilian's list of plants collected in the Missouri country, at the end of his work.

[69] *Populus balsamifera* the familiar cottonwood of the western plains. The French word gave a name to the great branch of the Mackenzie River.

[70] Blank in original.

[71] An old English remedy still in use.

great physician that I am plagered to cure every distemper in the camp. A man came today to me desiring me to act the man mid wife to his wife.

Sunday 14th. We remained the whole day here the Indians being busy with drying meat. I went a little distance up the River and saw a little Beaver work.

Monday 15th. We crossed the river at three different times in the Course of this days journey when it happened to intersect the line of our course which was S.S.W. and encamped on its borders about 14 miles higher up. It had the same appearance in every respect as when we arrived at it. The Indians Killed a few Beavers of which I got two dressed by my men to show them how to do it.

Tuesday 16th. We remained here the whole day. The Indians tried to dance the Bull dance in imitation of the B. Belly's but did it very ill.

Wednesday 17th. It rained in the morning, at 11 before noon the weather clearing up, we sat of following the river in a Course S.S. West about 9 miles. The bed and Banks in many places were solid Rock; there is very little water running. There is a few trees in the decline of the hill here.

Thursday 18th. I went hunting with the Chief while the camp flitted, we killed one cow and returned to the river at 3 in the after noon where we found the people encamped 15 miles S.W. of our last encampment. The banks and bed of the river are rocks; the plains are a continual series of high rocky hills whose sides and tops are partly covered with the red pine and other wood such as poplar, Elm, Ash, and a kind of Maple.

Fryday 19th. We [stopped] at an hour before sun set and encamped 5 miles higher up the river.

Saturday 20th. Some one being sick we did not stir. Here the point of the River was pretty large and well stocked with wood, viz. Liard, Ash and a kind of shrub resembling the prickly Ash which bears a fruit of the size of a small pea, red and of a sourish taste but not disagreeable.

Sunday 21st. The Camp rose at 8 in the morning and proceeded along the River for about 15 miles in a S.S. Westerly direction; the banks and bed of the river are of soil but muddy. I saw a beaver lying dead on the banks, here the river is fordable, without wetting ones feet in stepping over upon loose large stones, as we trotted almost the whole of this day's journey the unusual jolting of the Packages on the horses back occasioned the breaking of my thermometre. From this place we left the lesser Missouri on our left, its Course above this appears to be South to north, and stopping in the plains we encamped at one in the after noon on the side of a little river running into the lesser Missouri our course S.W. The Banks of L.M. [Lesser Missouri] in sight. We crossed two small Creeks in which there was no running water but many deep ponds in which there are Beavers. We saw this day plenty of Buffaloes.

We remained at this place 2 days. I have been very sick since some time, and so weak that it was difficult I could keep my saddle, the Indians on that occasion did not flit. I traded a few Beavers.

Thursday 25th. We sat of this morning at 10 following the little Creek on which we were encamped for 4 miles by a S.W. course and encamped. Wind S.E.

Fryday 26th. We passed through a Range of hills[72] whose tops and sides are covered with pine, and at the foot are many small creeks well wooded with Ash and Maple, there are plenty of different kinds of mint here which emit a very odoriferant smell. We crossed three small Creeks running north and N.W. into the Powder River[73] whose bancs we had in sight from the top of those hills. The wind was N.W. & very strong, a hurricane blew at night. The course we have pursued on a very barren soil for 22 Miles was West.

Saturday 27th. We arrived at noon at the Powder River after 6 hours ride by course West by South for about 20 miles. The Powder River is here about ¾ of an acre in breadth, its waters middling deep, but it appears to have risen lately as a quantity of leaves and wood was drifting on it. The points of the river are large with plenty of full grown trees, but no underwood, so that on our arrival we perceived diverse herds of Elk Deers[74] through the woods. There are Beaver dams all along the river. Three of these animals have been felled by our Indians.

When we arrived here the plains on the western side of the river were covered with Buffaloes and the bottoms full of Elk and Jumping deers[75] & Bears which last are mostly yellow and very fierce.[76] It is amazing how very barren the ground is between this and the lesser Missouri, nothing can hardly be seen but those *Corne de Raquettes*.[77] Our horses were nearly

[72] Powder River Mountains.

[73] A branch of the Yellowstone. Rises in Wyoming, among the Big Horn Mountains, and joins the Yellowstone about lat. 46° 46' N.

[74] *Cervus canadensis*, the American elk or wapiti. The French traders and trappers called it *la biche*; hence the lake of that name frequently mentioned in Henry's Journal.

[75]. Antelope (*Antilocapra americana*). See previous note.

[76] Grizzly bear (*Ursus horribilis*).

[77] Probably the dogwood (*Cornus*).

starved. There is grass in the woods but none in the plains which by the by might with more propriety be called hills, for though there is very little wood it is impossible to find a level spot of one or two miles in extent except close to the River. The current in that river is very strong and the water so muddy as to be hardly drinkable. The Indians say it is always so, and that is the reason they call it Powder River, from the quantity of drifting fine sand set in motion by the coast[78] wind which blinds people and dirtys the water. There are very large sand shoals along the river for several acres breadth and length, the bed of the river is likewise sand, and its Course North East.

Sunday 28th. We remained here the whole day to let the horses feed, the women were bussily employed in dressing and drying the skins of those animals that were Killed Yesterday. I traded one 3 Beavers and one Bear skin.

Monday 29th. We rose the Camp late in the evening and pitched the tents about 4 miles higher up the river having followed for that short space a course S.W.

Tuesday 30th. Early this morning we set out; the body of the people followed the river for about 17 miles S.W. while I with the Chief and a few others went hunting. We wounded Cabrio, Buffalo, and the large horned animal,[79] but did not Kill any, which made the Chief say that some one had thrown bad medicin[80] on our guns and that if he could Know him he would surely die.

The Country is very hilly about the river, but it does not appear to be so much so towards the North. About two miles above the encampment a range of high hills begins on the west side of the River, and Continues North for about 20 miles, when it appears to finish. The tongu River[81] is close on the other side of it. There is a parting ridge between the two Rivers.

I assended some very high hills on the side of which I found plenty of shells of the Cornu amonys Species[82] by some called snake shell, likewise a kind of shining stone[83] lying bare at the surface of the ground having to all

[78] Probably refers to the well-known Chinook winds.

[79] Mountain sheep or big-horn (*Ovis Montana*).

[80] The Indian always blames his non-success in hunting to some 'bad medicine.' See Mackenzie (Masson, I, 373.)

[81] Tongue river. The Indian name was (*Lazeka*).

[82] *Cornu Ammonis*, or Ammonite, a fossil cephalopod shell related to the nautilus. Popularly known as serpent stone or snake stone.

[83] Quartz.

appearance been left there by the rain water washing away the surrounding earth, they are of different size and form, of a Clear water Colour and reflect with as much force as a looking glass of its size. It is certainly those stones that have given the name of shining to that Mountain.[84] The hills are high, rugged and barren mostly Rocks with beds of loose red gravel on their tops or near it which being washed down by the rain water give the hills a redish appearance. On many hills a heape of calomid stone[85] among which some time I find pumice stone.

When we left the encampment this morning we were stopped by a party of their soldiers who would not allow us to proceed, as they intended to have a general hunt, for fear that we should rise the Buffaloes, but upon promise being made by the Chief whom I accompanied that he would not hunt in the way of the Camp, and partly on my account we were suffered to go on. We were however under the necessity of gliding away unperceived to prevent Jealousy.

Wednesday 31st. We sat out at 7 in the morning and proceeded up the River in a Southern course for about 13 miles and encamped about mid day; the weather being very warm and the wind from the south. I traded a few Beaver skins.

Thursday August 1st. Rain and thunder storm prevented our stirring this day. The water rose about 6 inches in the river and is as thick as mud. The current very swift.

Fryday 2nd. Last night some children playing at some distance from the Camp on the river, were fired at. The Camp was allarmed and watchers were set for the night but nothing appeared. It rained hard during most part of the night. We rose the Camp at one in the afternoon following the river for about 9 miles in a south course. The hills of the River are at a less distance from one another than they were here tofore. The bottoms or points of the river are not so large nor so well wooded and the grass entirely eat up by the Buffaloes and Elk.

Saturday 3rd. We sat out at sun rise and encamped at one in the afternoon having pursued a South Course with fare [fair] weather and a south east wind. We followed the River as usually; its bends are very short not exceeding two miles and many not one. The face of the Country indicates our approach to the large Mountains and to the heads of the

---

[84] Larocque's statement is scarcely probable. It seems more reasonable to suppose that the name—which must have first reached European ears through Indian report—had its origin in the brilliant, snow-capped peaks of the Rockies. See Thwaites' 'Rocky Mountain Exploration,' chap. II.
[85] Probably 'calumet' stone, or pipestone.

River.[86] A few Jumping [deer] or chevreuils[87] were Killed today. It has been very Cold these few nights.

Sunday 4th. We did not rise the Camp till late in the evening. In the morning we assended the hills of the River and saw the Rocky Mountains[88] not at a very great distance with Spy Glass, its clifts and hollows could be easly observed with the wood interspersed among the Rocks. We removed our camp about 4 miles higher up the River having pursued a S.E. Course.

Monday 5th. We had a thick fog in the morning, the night was so Cold that one Blanket could not Keep us warm enough to sleep, so that I purchased two Buffaloe Robes. About midday however it is generally very warm. We sat of at 7 and continued our way for about 12 miles by a south course along the River and with a north West wind. We arrived at the forks of the Pine River[89] which are assunder for about one mile, and encamped. The water in this River is clear and good issuing from the Mountains at a short distance from this, and is very cold, while that of the Powder River was so muddy that the Indians were under the necessity of making [holes] in the Beach and drink the water that gathered in them. We left this last mentioned river on our left where we went up the Pine River which is between 20 & 30 yards in breadth and runs over rocks. There is a rapid at every point and very little wood along its banks.

Tuesday 6th. We rose the Camp at 7 and proceeded upwards along the Pine River in a S. Western direction for 12 miles, having the Rocky Mountains ahead and in sight all day. The weather was foggy with a N.W. wind. An Indian shot another mans wife in the breast and wounded her dangerously. Jealousy was the occasion thereof. The Indian after inquire when I intend to depart. They appear to wish me to be off. I have 23 Beaver skins which they think a great deal, and more than we have occasion for. They thought that upon seeing the Rocky Mountains we would immediately depart as they cannot imagine what I intend to see in them. It is hard to make them understand by signs only, especially in this case for they do not want to understand.

---

[86] That is, of the Little Missouri.

[87] French for roe-deer (*Capreolus caprea*), otherwise roebuck.

[88] Lewis and Clark anticipated Larocque by a few weeks in their first view of the Rocky Mountains, but neither could claim the honour of discovery, La Vérendrye having achieved that distinction some sixty-two years before. Larocque has as a matter of fact only reached the Big Horn, an offshoot of the main range.

[89] The west abounded in Pine rivers and creeks. Larocque's Pine river does not appear elsewhere under that name. It is a branch of Powder river, having its source in the Big Horn range.

Francois Larocque

Wednesday 7th. We sat of at 6 and pitched the tents at 9 miles higher up the River having followed a South course. The Indians hunted and killed many Buffaloes and one cow came and took refuge among the horses where she were killed. At 5 in the evening we again flitted and encamped 5 miles higher up having pursued the same course as in the morning with a head wind.

Thursday 8th. We marched 24 miles in a south West course along the Pine River. Many small Branches fall in it at a little distance from one another. A man and horse were wounded by a Bear but not dangerously. There is much fruit here about and many Bears. Wind S.E. We are here encamped at the foot of the mountain.

Fryday 9th. The people went out hunting and returned with many skins to be dressed for tents. The weather is Cloudy and the wind south. Rapids succeed each other in the River here very fast and the current between is very swift running on a bed of Rocks.

Saturday 10th. Some Indians arrived from hunting and brought 9 Beavers which I traded for Beads. Weather the same as yesterday.

Sunday 11th. They are undetermined in what course to proceed from this place they have sent a party of young men along the Mountains Westerly and are to wait here until they return. They often enquire with anxious expectation of our departure when I intend to leave them and to day they were more troublesome than usual. What I have seen of their lands hitherto has not given me the satisfaction I look for [in] Beavers. I told them that I would remain with them 20 or 30 days more. That I wished very much to see the River aux Roches Jaunes[90] and the place they usually inhabit, otherwise that I would be unable to return and bring them their wants. They saw it was true, but to remove the objection of my not knowing their lands a few of them assembled and draughted on a dressed skin I believe a very good map of their Country[91] and they showed me the place where at different season they were to be found. The only reason I think they have in wishing my departure, is their haste to get what goods I still have. Besides we not a little embarrass the people in whose tent we live. They pretend to be fond of us, treat us well and say they will shed tears when we leave them.

[90] Yellowstone river. Rivière aux Roches Jaunes was the original French name, probably derived from some native equivalent.

[91] The Indian possesses a natural aptitude for map-making. Constant references are found in the narratives of explorers and furtraders to the skill and accuracy of these native geographers.

Monday 12th. In the evening the young men that had been sent to reconnoitre returned and reported that there was plenty of Buffaloes & fruit on the tongue and small horn River,[92] that they had seen a lately left encampment of their people who had not been at the Missouri (about 9 lodges) that they were gone across the Mountains that they had seen no appearance of their being enemies on that side. A Council ensued, and harangues were made to raise the Camp in the morning and proceed along to the River aux Roches Jaunes.

Tuesday 13th. We sat of at half after 8 in the morning following a West Course along the Mountain, through Creeks and hills such as I never saw before, it being impossible to climb these hills with Loaded Horses we were obliged to go round them about the middle of their hight from whence we were in imminent danger of rolling down being so steep that one side of the horses load rubbed against the side of the hill. One false step of the horse would certainly have been fatal to himself and rider. The wind was S.E. in the morning and north W. in the evening and the weather sultry. We encamped at 12 on the banks of a small branch of the Tongue River, whose water was very clear and cold as Ice. The people Killed two Bears to day. I traded a few Bears. I saw a few crows today which are the only birds I have seen since I left the Missouri except a few wood Peckers.

Wednesday 14th. It rained part of the morning, as soon as the rain ceased we sat off when it began again and continued raining until we reached another branch of the Tongue River, where we encamped. We went close along the mountain all the way for about 10 miles by a West Course crossing many small Creeks all running into the Tongue River, most of them were dry but thickly wooded with the Saule blanc;[93] there was no Beaver work I saw a few Cranes.

Thursday 15th. Fine clear weather. I traded 8 Beavers and purchased á horse for which I paid a gun 200 balls, one flanel Robe, one shirt, one half axe, one battle do, one bow iron, one comb, one But Knife, one small do, 2 Wampoon hair pipes, one......., 2 axes, one Wampoon shell, 40 B. Blue Beads, 2 Mass Barley Corn do and one fm W.S. Red Stroud.[94] We left this place at 11 before noon and proceeded 9 miles in a

[92] Lewis & Clark's Little Bighorn river.

[93] White willow.

[94] A coarse flannel blanket, made in Stroud, Gloucestershire, and very popular at one time in the Indian trade. In his Missouri Journal (Masson), Laroque mentions trading '1 fathom Hudson's Bay red strouds.' The initial letters are not clear in copy; may be 'W.S.', or 'U.S.', or 'U.T.'

North West Course and encamped on another branch of the Tongue River. Wind N.W. fine warm weather. The Indians Killed Buffaloes and a few Bears, the latter they hunt for pleasure only as they do not eat the flesh but in case of absolute necessity. Perhaps the whole nation is employed about a bear, whom they have caused to take refuge in a thicket, there they plague him a long while and then Kill him, he is seldom stript of his skin.

Fryday 16th. I purchased a saddle and [bridle?] for the horse I purchased yesterday for which I paid 40 shots Powder Being short of Balls. I gave 20 pounds Powder only for a Beaver 1 Knife, I sell 2 Beavers 10 String Blue Beads, 1 Beaver & so on. We proceeded along the mountain as usual by a N.W. Course about 15 miles, crossed 3 small Creeks emptying in the Tongue River where we arrived at one in the afternoon,[95] we forded it and encamped on the north side, N. & N.E. is a small Mountain lying between this river and the large Horn River, they call it the Wolf Teeth.[96] (Se la is in the Rocky Mountain language and Seja in the Big Belly's.) Fine weather wind N.W.

Saturday 17th. The Indians having hunted yesterday we did not rise the Camp but remained here all day. There were many Bears here about, who are attracted by the quantity of Choak Cherries[97] and other fruit there is here. The Woods along the Rivers are as thickly covered with Bears Dung as a Barn door is of that of the Cattle, large Cherry trees are broken down by them in Great number. The Indians Kill one or two almost every day. The Tongue River here is small being only about 20 feet broad with two feet water in the deepest part of the rapids. It receives many additional small stream in its way to the River Roches Jaunes. The points of the River are pretty large and well stocked with wood viz....[98] & maple.

Sunday 18th. At 7 o'clock we left our encampment and proceeded Northward; at noon we stopped on a branch of the small Horn River & the greatest part of the Indians went on to the small Horn River to hunt. At half past two in the afternoon we sat off again and crossing the River we encamped on its Borders where we found the hunting party with their

[95] Not far north of the boundary between Montana and Wyoming.

[96] Tongue river flows through a small range known as Chetish or Wolf Mountains. Another small range, Rosebud Mountains, lies between Tongue river and the Big Horn. Either might be Larocque's 'Wolf Teeth.'

[97] The choke-cherry (*Prunus Virginiana*) is found everywhere on the Upper Missouri and Yellowstone.

[98] Name of some other tree omitted here.

horses loaded with fresh meat. We travelled about 15 miles this day and are farther from the mountain than yesterday though still close to it.

Monday 19th. Since we are close to the mountain many women have deserted with their lovers to their fine tents that are across the mountain, there are no Cattle in the mountain nor on the other side, so that they are loth to go that way, while the desertion of their wives strongly Call them there. Harangues were twice made to rise the Camp, and counter order were given before the tents were thrown down. The reason of this is that the wife of the Spotted Crow who regulates our mo[ve]ments has deserted, he is for going one way while the Chief of the other bands are for following our old course. Horses have been Killed and women wounded since I am with them on the score of jealousy.[99] Today a snake Indian shot his wife dead but it seems not without reason for it is said it was the third time he found her and the Gallant together. The Small Horn river runs East from the Mountain to this place here it makes a bend N by East and passing round of the wolf teeth it falls into the large Horn river. The bed of the River here is Rocks a continual rapid, the water clear and cold as Ice, the ground barren and the banks of the river thinly wooded with same Kind of wood as heretofore. I traded 6 Beavers.

Tuesday 20th. We flitted and encamped 3 miles higher up the River on a beautiful spot where there was plenty of fine grass for the horses, our Course West. I traded 3 Beavers.

Wednesday 21st. I made a present of a few articles to the Chief and a few other Considered Persons. We remained here all day. There is plenty of ash here. There were very few persons in the Camp that were not employed in making themselves horse whip handles with that wood; it was with that design they came here, as that wood is seldom found elsewhere. I saw some Beavers work on that River.

Thursday 22nd. Water frose the thickness of paper last night in horsetracks. I was called to a Council in the Chiefs Brothers tent Lodge, where the Spotted Crow resigned his employment of regulating our marches, an other old man took the office upon himself and told me that he intended to pursue their old course to the River aux Roches Jaune. I traded 8 Beavers with the Snake Indians in whose possession I saw a Kettle or Pot hewn out of a solid stone, it was about 1½ inch thick & contained about 6 or 8 quarts; it had been made with no other instrament but a piece of Iron.

[99] See previous note.

Fryday 23rd. We rose the Camp at 11 in the forenoon and followed a N.E. Course for one mile N.W. 6 de, & encamped on a branch of the....[100] River, where there is a Beaver Dam and other work occasionally found. I traded—4 Beavers. Wind S.E. the only roads practicable to Cross the mountain are at the heads of this and the Tongue River.

Saturday 24th. This morning we were allarmed by the report that three Indians had been seen on the first hill of the mountain and that three Buffaloes were in motion and that two shots had been heard towards the large Horn River. Thirty men saddled their horses and immediately went off to see what was the matter while all the other Kept in readiness to follow if necessary. In a few hours some came back and told us that they had seen 35 on foot walking on the banks of one of the branches of the Large Horn River. In less time than the Courrier Could well tell his news no one remained in the Camp, but a few old men and women, all the rest scampered off in pursuit. I went along with them we did not all Set off together nor could we all Keep together as some horses were slower than others but the foremost stopped galloping on a hill, and continued on with a small trot as people came up. They did the dance[101] when the Chief arrived, he and his band or part of it galloped twice before the main body of the people who still continued their trot intersecting the line of their course while one of his friends I suppose his aide de Camp harangued. They were all dressed in their best Cloths. Many of them were followed by their wives who carried their arms, and who were to deliver them at the time of Battle. There were likewise many children, but who could Keep their saddles. Ahead of us were some young men on different hills making signs with their Robes which way we were to go.[102] As soon as all the Chiefs were come up and had made their harangue every one set off the way he liked best and pursued according to his own judgement. The Country is very hilly and full of large Creeks whose banks are Rocks so that the pursued had the advantage of being able to get into places where it was impossible to go with horses & hide themselves. All escaped but two of the foremost who being scouts of the party had advanced nearer to us than the others and had not discovered us, they were surrounded after a long race but Killed and scalped in a twinkling. When I arrived at the dead bodies they had taken but his scalp and the fingers of his right hand with which

---

[100] Name illegible.
[101] War dance. See Maximilian, II, 291, *et seq*.
[102] Maximilian, III, 300, *et seq* — Notes on Indian Sign Language.

the outor was off. The[y] Borrowed my hanger with which the[y] cut off his left hand and returned it [the knife] to me bloody as a mark of honour and desired me to.......at him. Men women and children were thronging to see the dead Bodies and taste the Blood. Everyone was desirous of stabbing the bodies to show what he would have done had he met them alive and insulted & frotted at them in the worst language they could give. In a short time the remains of a human body was hardly distinguishable. Every young man had a piece of flesh tied to his gun or lance with which he rode off to the Camp singing and exultingly showing it to every young woman in his way, some women had whole limb dangling from their saddles. The sight made me Shudder with horror at such Cruelties and I returned home in quite [a] different frame from that in which I left it.

Sunday 25th. The Scalp dance was danced all night and the scalps carried in procession through the day.

Monday 26th. It rained in the morning as it did yesterday, at noon the Weather Clearing we sat off Course S.W. wind S.E. fine weather. We encamped in the mountain 9 miles distant from our last encampment by a small Creek in which there was little running water, but an amazing number of Beaver Dams. I counted 6 in about 2 points of the River but most of them appeared to be old Dams. The young men paraded all day with the scalps tied to their horses bridles sing[ing] and keeping time with the Drum and Sheskequois[103] or Rattle.

Tuesday 27th. We remained here all day, 10 Young Men were sent to observe the motions of those who were routed lately, they are afraid of being attacked having seen the road of a numerous body of people on the large Horn River. In the evening news came that the Buffaloes were in motion on the Large Horn River, and harangues were made to guard the Camp.

Wednesday 28th. Two hours before day light, all the Indians horses were saddled at their doors, they put all their young children on horse back & tied to the saddles, then they slept the remainder of the night. They likewise loaded some horses with the most valuable part of their property while they in the expectation of being attacked sat in the tents their arms ready & their horses saddled at the door. At broad day light nothing appearing they took in their children and unloaded their horses. At 9 in

---

[103] Catlin calls the rattle She-she-quois, and says 'that most generally used is made of rawhide, charged with pebbles, which produce a shrill noise to mark time in the Indian dances and songs.' See two illustrations on Plate 101½, p. 210, Catlin, I.

the morning 4 young men arrived and reported that they had seen nothing of the enemy, that there were party Buffaloes between the Large Horn and the River aux Roches Jaunes.

Thursday 29th. We rose the Camp this morning and marched a Course West by North. The Indians hunted and saw Strange Indians. There was a Continual harangue by different Chiefs the whole night which with the singing and dancing of the scalp prevented any Sleep being had. We pitched the tents on a small creek running into the large Horn River distant about 20 miles from our last encampment.

Fryday 30th. We left the place and encamped on the Large Horn River close to the foot of the mountain and of very high Rocks. Course West about 5 miles.

Saturday 31st. We remained at this place the whole day. Some young one who had been en découverte returned from a deserted camp of about 30 Lodges where they found Chief Coats N.B. straud[104] Wampoon shells and other articles, which it seems had been left by the people inhabiting those tents upon some panic. This is what these Indians say but it is my opinion that those goods are rather an offering to the supreme being which those Indians often make and leave in tree well wrapt up, and which our young men found. This River is broad deep and clear water strong courrent, bed stone and gravel about ½ mile above this encampment, the River runs between 2 big Rocks & loses ⅔ of its breadth but gains proportionally in depth. There is no beach at the foot of the Rocks, they are but perpendicular down to the water. It is aweful to behold and makes one giddy to look down upon the river from the top of those Rocks.[105] The River appears quite narrow and runs with great rapidity immediately under our feet, so that I did not dare to look down but when I could find a stone behind which I could keep & looking over it to see the foaming water without danger of falling in. This river does not take its rise in this mountain, it passes through the mountains and takes its water in the next range.[106] There is a fall in this River 30 or 40 miles above this where presides a Manitoin[107] or Devil. These Indians say it is a Man

[104] Stroud, *i.e.* cloth or blanket.

[105] The description would seem to point to the Big Horn Cañon, but Larocque's narrative makes it clear that he was farther down the river.

[106] The Big Horn river rises in Western Wyoming, in the main range of the Rocky Mountains. It flows around the northwestern extremity of the Big Horn range.

[107] Manitou, or more properly, Windego. Scores of waterfalls have been the reputed home of this picturesque but rather bloodthirsty spirit. In one form or another, and under varying names, the Windego ranged almost from the Atlantic to the Pacific.

Wolf who lives in the fall and rises out of it to devour any person or beast that go to near. They say it is impossible to Kill him for he is ball proof. I measured a Ram's horn which I found when walking along the River, it was 5 spans in length and was very weighty, it seems to me that the animal who carried it died of old age for the small end of the horn was much worn and broke into small splinters, which was not the case in any of the animals I saw Killed, nor were their horns of that size neither.

The Mountain is here a solid Rock in most places bare and naked, in other places Cloathed with a few Red Pine. The sides of some Coulé are as smooth and perpendicular as any wall, and of an amazing hight; and in places there are holes in those perpendicular Rocks resembling much those niches in which statues are placed. Others like church doors & vaults, the tout ensemble is grand and striking. Beautiful prospects are to be had from some parts of those Rocks, but the higher places are inaccessible. The Large Horn River is seen winding through a level plain of about 3 miles breadth for a great distance almost to its conflux with the River aux Roches Jaunes.

Sunday, September 1st. We Left this place and pitched our tents about 3 miles lower down where we remained two days, while we were here a Snake Indian arrived, he had been absent since the Spring and had seen part of his nation who traded with the Spaniards, he brought a Spanish B[r]idle and Battle ax, a large thick blanket, striped white and black and a few other articles, such as Beads, etc. A Missouri Big Belly fished here and cought 14 moyens Cat fish[108] in a very short time.

We had much dancing at this place still for the scalps. There are Islands in the River here but most of them are heaps of sand. The Wooded points of the River do not join the open plain is seen between them but there is plenty of wood in some places. The leaves beg[in] to fall.

Wednesday 4th. We left the encampment and proceeded N.W. by North about 15 miles and pitched the tents on a Small Creek running into the Large Horn River. Where we left the River we had a level plain for about 4 or 5 miles when the Country became hilly and barren.

Thursday 5th. We Kept the same Course as yesterday and encamped on a most small Creek running as the former about the same nature.

Fryday 6th. We rose the Camp early and at 11 before noon arrived at Mampoa or Shot stone River,[109] from whence the Indians went out to

---

[108] *Amiurus nebulosus.* Moyen catfish, *I.E.*, middle-sized catfish.

[109] Manpoa or Shot Storm river, Larocque spells it farther on. Shannon's Creek, a small tributary of the Yellowstone.

hunt, there being plenty of Buffaloes on the road to this place, the mountains were as follows. The mountain along which we travelled from the Pine River lay S.E. another called Amanchabé Clije south, the Boa [or Bod] Mountain S.W. but appeared faintly on account of a thick fog that covered it.

Saturday 7th. We remained all day here, the Indian women being very bussy to dry tongues and the best part of the meat and dressing skins for a great feast they are preparing while their war exploits are recapitulated.

Sunday 8th. I sat off early this morning with two Indians to visit the River aux Roches Jaunes and the adjacent part. I intended to return from this place as the Indians will take a very round about road to go there. We were not half ways, when we fell in with Buffaloes, my guides were so bent upon hunting that they did not guide me where I wanted, and we returned at night to the tents with meat, but with rain as it rained from noon till night. The Indians showed me a mountain lying North West which they told me was in direct line to the Missouri falls and not far from it.[110] We passed through two new raised Camps of strange Indians at the door of the largest tent were 7 heaps of sticks each containing 10 sticks denoting the number of lodges in the Camp, to have been 70.

Monday 9th. I purchased a horse we had information that four strangers had been seen who likewise saw our people & hid themselves. At night a young man arrived who saw and conversed (I cannot say he spoke for the whole conversation was carried on by signs they not understanding one another language) with a fort de prairie Big Belly,[111] they wanted to bring each other to their respective Camps but both were afraid and neither of them dared to go to the other Camp. The B.B. are encamped on the large Horn River behind the mountain and are come on peaceable terms they are 275 or 300 Lodges.

Tuesday 10th. We rose the Camp at 9 and took a N. West Course to the River aux Roches Jaunes where we arrived[112] at two in the afternoon distant 16 miles we forded into a large Island in which we encamped. This is a fine large River in which there is a strong current, but the Indians say there are no falls. Fordable places are not easly found although I believe the water to be at its lowest. The bottoms are large and well wooded.

[110] Some error here, as the Great Falls of the Missouri are about 200 miles in an air line from where Larocque then stood.

[111] The Fall Indians of the Saskatchewan, (*Atsinas*).

[112] He reached the Yellowstone below Pryor's Fork.

Wednesday 11th. 5 Big Bellys arrived and came into our lodge being the Chief Lodge. They brought words of peace from their nation and say they Come to trade horses. They were well received by the Indians and presents of different articles were made them. They told me they had traded last winter with Mr. Donald whom they made Known to me a[s] crooked arm.[113] I went round the Island in which we are encamped, it is about 5 miles in circumference and thickly wooded in some places all along the North Side of the Island. The Beaver has cut down about 50 feet of the wood. 9 Lodges of the people that were left in the Spring was joined in they are 15 tents at present, they encamped on the opposite side of the River.

Thursday 12th. I traded six large Beavers from the Snake Indians. We crossed from the Island to the West side of the River & proceeded upward for about 9 miles south West and encamped in a point where they usually make their fall medicine.

Fryday 13th. I bought a Horn Bow & a few Arrows a Saddle &[114] pichimom,[115] part of a tent and a few of those blue Glass Beads they have from the Spaniards, and on which they set such value that a horse is given for 100 grains.

Saturday 14th. Having now full filled the instructions I received from Mr. Chaboillez, which were to examine the lands of the Crow Indians and see if there is Beaver as was reported, and I to invite them to hunt it, I now prepared to depart, I assembled the Chiefs in Council, and after having smoked a few pipes, I informed them that I was setting off, that I was well pleased with them and their behaviour towards me, and that I would return to them next fall. I desired them to kill Beavers and Bears all winter for that I would come and trade with them and bring them their wants. I added many reasons to show them that it was their interest to hunt Beavers, and then proceeded to settle the manners of Knowing one

[113] John McDonald of Garth, known among the fur-traders and Indians as 'Bras Croche' because of his deformed arm. McDonald wrote a series of exceedingly interesting Autobiographical Notes, 1791-1816, for which see Masson, II, 1-59. They were written at the age of 85, and are consequently not always to be relied upon in the matter of dates. He says that he built New Chesterfield House (on South Saskatchewan, at mouth of Red Deer) in 1805, and gives a graphic account of the arrival of a band of 'Missisourie Indians' (evidently the 'Big Bellys' whom Larocque now mentions) about Christmas of that year. Larocque's Journal makes it clear that the year should be 1804.

[115] Or, pichimori, copy is indistinct. Possibly the Crow name for a bridle. It may even be a very wild spelling or transcription of pemmican, the mixture of pounded meat and melted fat which formed so important a feature of the fur-traders' equipment.

[114] Saddle cloth apichimon. See note in first part of this pamphlet.

another next fall, and how I am to find them which is as follows. Upon my arrival at the Island if I do not find them I am to go to the Mountain called Amanchabé Chije & then light 4 dift fires on 4 successive days, and they will Come to us (for it is very high and the fire can be seen at a great distance) in number 4 & not more, if more than four come to us we are to act upon the defensive for it will be other Indians. If we light less than 3 fires they will not come to us but think it is enemies. They told me that in winter they were always to be found at a Park by the foot of the Mountain a few miles from this or there abouts. In the spring and fall they are upon this River and in summer upon the Tongue and Horses[116] River.

I have 122 Beavers 4 Bears and two otters which I traded not so much for their value (for they are all summer skins) as to show them that I set some value on the Beavers and our property. The presents I made them I thought were sufficient to gain their good will in which I think I succeeded.

I never gave them any thing without finding means to let them know it was not for nothing. Had more been given they would have thought that good[s] were so common among us than to set no value upon them, for Indians that have seen few White men will be more thankful for a few articles given them than for great many, as they think that little or no value is attached to what is so liberally given. It was therefore I purchased their Bears and likewise as a proof that there is Beaver in those parts, besides it saved to distribute the good I had into the most deserving hands, that is the less lazy.

We departed about noon 2 Chiefs accompanied us about 8 miles, we stopped and smoked a parting pipe, the[y] embrased us, we shook hands & parted they followed us about one mile, at a distance gradually lessening their steps till we were almost out of sight and Crying or pretending to Cry they then turned their backs and went home. At parting they promissed that none of their young men would follow us, they took heaven and earth to witness to attest their sincerity in what they had told us, and that they had opened their ears to my words and would do as I desired them, they made me swear by the same that I would return and that I told them no false words (and certainly I had no intention of breaking my oath nor have I still. If I do not keep them my word it certainly is not my fault).

Our course was N.E. 20 miles, a little before sun set we were overtaken by a storm which forced us into a point of the River where we

---

[116] Possibly, Pumpkin creek, the chief branch of Tongue river.

encamped & passed the night during which our horses were frightened & it was with difficulty we could get them together again. We Kept watch by night.

Sunday 15th. We followed a N.E. course and crossed the River Roches Jaunes at 9 and proceeded along the South side, at 10 we crossed Manpoa River at its entrance into River Roches Jaunes, Manpoa or the Shot Storm River is about 10 feet in breadth and with very little water it take its waters in Amanabe Chief at a short distance there is wood along its Banks, especially close to the mountain and Beaver on the east side of this River, close to its discharge in the River Roches Jaunes is a Whitish perpendicular Rock on which is painted with Red earth a battle between three persons on horseback and 3 on foot,[117] at 2 in the afternoon we arrived at a high hill on the side of the river called by the Natives Erpian Macolié where we stopped to refresh our horses & killed one Cow. An hour before sun set we sat of again and encamped after dark making no fire for fear of being discovered by horse thieves or enemies. From Manpoa to this p[l]ace our Course was east. Buffaloes and Elk we found in great plenty. Wind S.W.

Monday 16th. It froze hard last night North, Weather Cloudy N.E. 9 miles and stopped to Cook victuals for the day as we make no fire at night. Elk and Buffaloes in the greatest plenty. It rained till 3 in the afternoon, when weather clearing we sat off and encamped at the Rocks of the large Horn River where we arrived at 8 in the evening.

Tuesday 17th. We crossed the river early in the morning, its points here are large & beautiful well stocked with wood, we passed through a most abominable Country and often despaired of being able to get clear of this place enceting (*sic*) with Rocks which it was impossible to ascend or to go round so we were obliged often to go back on other road which presented us with the same difficulties, at last we ascended the hill but

---

[117] Descending the Yellowstone, in July, 1806, Captain Clark visited a remarkable rock near the confluence of Shannon's Creek with the Yellowstone. He describes it as 'nearly four hundred paces in circumference, two hundred feet high, and accessible only from the northeast, the other sides being a perpendicular cliff of a light-coloured gritty rock. The Indians have carved the figures of animals and other objects on the sides of the rock, and on the top are raised two piles of stones.' He named this remarkable rock Pompey's pillar, and it is so marked on his map. This is apparently the same rock mentioned by Laroque, and his Manpoa river is Clark's Shannon's creek.

being on the top did not offer a more pleasing prospect, we were often obliged to unload the horses and carry baggage ourselves and the horses being light we made chump [jump] over.....[118] in the Rock and climb precipices, but were near losing then at last at 3 in the afternoon we passed the whole of that bad road and arrived at the Border of Rocks where we could see a fine level country before us but the sun was set before we could find a practiable road to come down to it, which we effected not without unloading the horses and carrying down their loads part of the way, while the horses slided down upon their rumps about 25 yards. We broke some of our saddles, and arrived in the plain just as the day was setting and encamped further on by the side of the River. It is probable that had we had a guide with us we could have avoided those Rocks, while our ignorance of the Road made us enter into & once engaged among the difficulty was as great to return as to proceed. We Kept no regular course, but went on as we could to all points of the compass in order to extricate ourselves. We Killed one Elk.

Wednesday 18th. This morning we saw the points of wood where we encamped last night 9 miles south of us from which we were parted by the River on one side and the Rocks on the other. I heard the noise of the fall or Great Rapids[119] yesterday, but now at too great a distance from the River and too busily engaged to go and see it. It froze hard last night, we left our encampment later our horses were tired, but after having set out did not stop till after sun set having followed for 22 miles a north East course wind South West. Fine weather plenty Elk and Buffaloes.

Thursday 19th. Cold and Cloudy and followed the same course as last day for 22 miles stopped at 2 in the afternoon and Killed a stag which was very poor being its Rutting Season. We resumed our course to the N. East for 8 miles and encamped for the night.

Friday 20th. We sat this day early out, assended the hills which are rugged and barren proceeding N.E. for 36 miles. Killed one large..., fine weather with a N.E. wind.

Saturday 21st. We had a very bad road. Came down to the River to see if we could find a better passage but it was impossible, the River striking the Rock at every bend and assended the hill again and with difficulty made our way over Rocks. After sun set we encamped on the

[118] Illegible, may be 'channels,' in sense of chasms.

[119] Not clear to what falls Larocque refers. The Yellowstone is navigable from its mouth to some distance above Larocque's present position.

River a la Langue[120] Killed 2 Elks which were very fat. Course East for 18 miles wind N.E.

Sunday 22nd. We crossed the River a la Langue and passed over a plain of about 9 miles in breadth where we came again to Rocks and precipices without number over which we jogged on without stopping till 2 hours before sun set when we encamped on the side of the River close to a Rapid. There is little or no wood here along the River except a few Liards scattered here and there and no grass at all. Course N.E. for about 18 miles. Wind S.W.

Monday 23rd. We had a pretty level plain the whole of the day 12 miles West and 24 miles N.E. At 10 we crossed the Powder River,[121] it has no wood on its bank here and is much shallower than when we crossed it going; its water is the same being still muddy, we encamped at night by a small Creek, having been unable to find grass for our horses throughout the day we were obliged to cut down three Lair[d]s and let the horses feed on the bark.

Tuesday 24th. Set off early, at 9 in the morning we found a place where there was grass where we stopped and let our horses eat. At three in the afternoon we saddled our horses and went on until we encamped after sunset having followed an Eastern Course for 13 miles. Wind S.W. fine weather. It is 4 nights since it froze.

Wednesday 25th. We passed through a very uneven country, but there being no Rocks we had no very great difficulties and encamped at night in a very large point of wood in which there was plenty of Deer — watched all night having seen something like a man Creeping on the beach. We had made this day 37 miles by a North Course. The fire is in the plains from which the wind brought columns of thick smoke in abundance so that we could barely see. We shoed our horses with raw deer hide as their hoofs are worn out to the flesh with continual walking since last Spring setting their feet on loose stones lames then & sometimes makes them bleed.

Thursday 26th. What we saw last night and mistook for a man was a Bear whose tracks we found this morning. We sat out at 8 and the plain being even we went on at a great rate, at 2 in the afternoon we stopped to Kill a cow, our provision being out, at three we sat off again and met on our road a female bear eating....we killed her and took the skin it being good. At five we stopped for the night.

[120] Tongue River. See previous note.

[121]. Crosses Powder River about midway between the forks and mouth.

<h1 style="text-align:center">Francois Larocque</h1>

Here the River is divided into many channels forming so many islands,[122] the banks and islands are thickly covered with woods, chiefly Liard, oak and maple. Our course was North which followed for 39 miles having the wind ahead, which brought us thick smoke in abundance. We saw this day plenty Elk and Buffaloes.

Fryday 27th. We crossed a plain of about 6 miles and arrived at a bend of the River where it was impossible to continue on the hill so that we were fain to descend to the River and Beach. We bemired 3 of our horses and got them out but with great difficulty. At one we stopped to let the horses eat. The wind was south and we had no appearance of smoke but the weather threatened rain. We encamped at sun set after having followed a North course for 24 miles and found plenty of grass.

Saturday 28th. This whole day we travelled through a level country having fine weather. We made 30 miles in a Northerly direction and passed 3 Indian encampment of this summer, whom I suppose must have been occupied by warriors for the[y] had no tents.

Sunday 29th. We passed through a most beautiful and pleasant country, the river being well wooded. We found here more fine grass than in any place since I left the Missouri and of course the greatest number of Buffaloes. The wind was N.W. and the weather Cloudy and Cold. Having made 30 miles by a N.N.E. Course we encamped on a small creek round which the river passed.

Monday 30th. We assended the hill which produces plenty of fine grass; about 6 miles further we saw the forks of the River aux Roches Jaunes and the Missouri Course N.E. 27 miles and descended to the River (the Missouri) having but a bend. We had followed the River for 7 miles when we heard the report of a gun twice, and the voice of a woman as crying. We stopped and sent Morrison[123] en decouverte and I and Souci remained to watch the horses and property. Morrison returned in about 2 hours and reported that what we had taken for a Woman's voice was that of a young Cub, and as to the gun we supposed it proceeded from trees thrown down by the wind, as it blew very hard, and the Buffaloes, Bears and Elk were very quiet in the wood and plain, so that there was no appearance of being any human Creature there about. We went on & assended the hills to cut a large bend of the River following an east course for 11 miles and encamped in a large point of Elm trees for the night. The

---

[122] See description of this portion of the Yellowstone, in Lewis & Clark II, chap. 17.

[123] William Morrison. See Masson's Liste des Bourgeois, &c., I, 402, 403.

Wind was North West and very strong tearing down trees by their roots every moment.

Tuesday October 1st. Weather Cloudy raining now and then, Wind N.W. very cold Course North 12 miles. Passing through a Coulé yesterday I found a lodge made in the form of those of the Mandans & Big Bellys (I suppose made by them) surrounded by a small Fort. The Lodge appears to have been made 3 or 4 years ago but was inhabited last winter. Outside of the fort was a Kind of Stable in which the[y] kept their horses. There was plenty of Buffaloes heads in the Fort some of them painted red.

Wednesday 2nd. Strong N.W. wind Cold and Cloudy—Course N.E. 26 miles Killed a Cow—Country even plenty of grass.

Thursday 3rd. Set off at 7 through a very hilly and bad country N.E. 20 miles east 15 and encamped on the River it rained part of the day Wind north West very Cold.

Fryday 4th. It rained and was bad weather all night, at break of the day it began to snow and continued snowing very hard ·till 2 in the afternoon. Strong N.W. wind. We sought our horses all day without being able to find them till after sun set; the bad weather having drawn them in the woods.

Saturday 5th. Sat off early, fine weather Course S.E. by E. 26 miles plenty of Buffaloes on both sides of the River. Killed Cow.

Sunday 6th. All the small Creeks and Ponds were frozen over this morning Course S.E. by S. 20 miles Sout[h]—passed through a thick wood of about 4 miles.

Monday 7th. East 2 miles south 11 we arrived at the lesser Missory which we crossed S.E. 3 miles saw many Bears and Skunks.

Tuesday 8th. Assended the hills, Plains even 39 miles S.S.E. fine warm weather wind S.W.

Wednesday 9th. Proceeded on the hills through a fine Country course E. by S. 12 miles. South 2 miles and arrived at the Big Bellys who were encamped about 3 miles above their village. I found here a letter of Mr. Charles McKenzie to me.

Thursday 10th. I remained here all day to refresh the horses before I proceed to the Assinibois River. Among other news the Indians tell me that there are 14 American Crafts below the [villages?] who are ascending to this place.[124] The Sioux have Killed 8 White men last spring upon St. Peters River & 3 Big Bellys here.

[124] This would seem to refer to the Lewis & Clark Expedition, but at this date Lewis & Clark were on Columbian waters west of the Rocky Mountains.

Francois Larocque

Fryday 11th. I intended crossing over today but was prevented by the strength of the wind which blew all day with amazing violence from the North West. I got a few pair of shoes made and Corn pounded for provision, news came that the Sioux were seen encamped at a short distance below. Expecting to be attacked they [the Big Bellies] were under arms all night.

Saturday 12th. About noon the weather being calm & warm we crossed the River; the horses swam the whole bredth of the River & were nearly spent. We met with 3 Assiniboines and their wives on the North side of the River who were going to the Big Bellys to trade. We went slowly on till sun set when we encamped on the side of a small lake in the Plains which are burning to the West. Course North.

Sunday 13th. Fine weather, wind N.W. plenty of ......[125] Buffaloes just arriving in the plain. Few being on all sides. The Buffaloes were in motion so that we could not get near enough to get a shot at them, & our horses so tired & fatigued that I did not chuse to run them. We crossed the fire at sun set and encamped by the side of a small lake whose borders had escaped the general Conflagration.

Monday 14th. We watched our horses all that night for fear of Assiniboines, of whom we had seen the tracks, in the evening; sat off before sun rise and arrived at 10 in the forenoon at the River la Sourie where we stopped for the remainder of the day. The grass on either side of the river here is not burnt but the fire appears on both sides at a distance, West and north. Soon in the evening the Buffaloes were in motion on the North side of the River which made us fear for our horses.[126]

Tuesday 15th. After dark last night we left our encampment and mar[ched] two and a half hours by star light, when Clouds gathering so as to obscure our sight of the stars and of course being unable to regulate our course we stopped in a Creek and there passed the night being free of anxiety.

In the morning we proceeded weather Cold and Cloudy wind N.W. We stopped for the Night on the deep River,[127] which does not draw the name of a Riper, being a hallow .....[128] in the plain in which there are

---

[125] In this and in other cases of omitted words throughout the journal the lacuna is in the Laval University copy, of which this is a transcription.

[126] The movement of the buffaloes suggesting the presence of those dreaded horse-thieves of the Assiniboines.

[127] Some small creek, not now distinguishable.

[128] Word illegible.

small deep ponds communicating with each other in the spring and rainy seasons only, nor is there a single twig to be found about. At sun set it began to rain and continued so all night. We covered the property with part of a tent we had, and we passed the whole night Shivering by a small fire made of Cowdung[129] (which we had taken care to gather before the rain began) with the assistance of our saddle on our back, by the way of Cloaks.

Wednesday 16th. It snowed rained and hailed the whole day. Wind N.W. and amazing strong. We arrived after dark at the woods of one of the Elk Head Rivers,[130] wet to the skin and quite benumbed with Cold.

Thursday 17th. Weather Cloudy and wind N.W. and very Cold so we were fain to stop, make a fire and warm ourselves, especially as we are not over and above well dressed to Keep off the Cold. We wrapt ourselves in Buffaloe Robes and proceeded to the Grand Coulé[131] and encamped on the very same spot where we had the quarrel last spring with the Assiniboine.

Fryday 18th. In the morning we met with a few Assiniboines coming from the Fort, we stopped and smoked a pipe with them. They told us that Mount a la Bosse [fort] had been evacuated[132] and that Mr. Falcon[133] was building a house to winter in,[134] about half ways between that and R. qu'il appelle Fort.[135] We arrived at Mount a la Bosse Fort, where I found Mr. Charles McKenzie and 3 men taking care of the remaining property.

I remained here one day and then went to see Mr. Falcon at the Grand Bois about 15 miles above this, returned the next day and then sat out for River la Sourie Fort[136] where I arrived the 22 October. So ends my Journal of my Journey to the Rocky Mountains.

---

[129] The *bois de vache*, or 'bodevache' (probably a corruption of *bouse de vache*), so often mentioned in the journals of western fur-traders. This unsatisfactory fuel had often to be resorted to in crossing the prairie, where wood of any kind was unprocurable.

[130] North and South Antler creeks. North Antler creek was formerly called Tete a la Biche.

[131] Near Souris river, north or northwest of Turtle Mountain.

[132] This is important as fixing the date of the abandonment of the Montagne à la Bosse post, which has hitherto been in doubt.

[133] Pierre Falcon. Se Masson's *Liste* under 'Haut de la Rivière Rouge.' He was father of the Half-Breed of the same name who took part in the Seven Oaks affair when Governor Semple met his death, and was the author of a ballad on the fight, for which see Hargrave's 'Red River,' p. 488. See Tassé's 'Canadiens de l'Ouest,' II, 339, *et seq*.

[134] Grand Bois, as Larocque names it in the following paragraph.

[135] Rivière Qu'Appelle Fort, at the mouth of the river of same name, an affluent of the Assiniboine.

[136] On the south side of the Assiniboine, at the mouth of the Souris river.

Francois Larocque

A FEW OBSERVATIONS ON THE ROCKY MOUNTAIN INDIANS WITH WHOM I PASSED THE SUMMER, 1805.

This nation known among the Sioux by the name of Crow Indians inhabit the Eastern part of the Rocky Mountains at the head of the River aux Roches Jaunes (which is Known by the Kinistinaux and Assiniboines by the name of River a la Biche, from the great number of Elks with which all the Country along it abounds) and its Branches and Close to the head of the Missouri.

There are three principal tribes of them whose names in their own language are *Apsarechas, Kee the resas* and *Ashcabcaber*, and these tribes are again divided into many other small ones[1] which at present consist but of very few people each, as they are the remainder of a numerous people who were reduced to their present number by the ravage of the Small Pox, which raged among them for many years successively and as late as three years ago. They told me they counted 2000 Lodges or tents in their Camp when alltogether before the Small Pox had infected them. At present their whole number consist of about 2400 persons dwelling in 300 tents and are able to raise 600 Warriors like the Sioux and Assiniboines. They wander about in Leather tents and remain where there are Buffaloes and Elks. After having remained a few days in one place so that game is not more so plentiful as it was they flit to another place where there are Buffaloes or deers and so on all the year around. Since the great decrease of their numbers they generally dwell all together and flit at the same time and as long as it is possible for them to live when together they seldom part. The fear of some of their neighbours with whom they are at war compels them to that, as collectively they can repulse a greater party of their

---

[1] Lewis H. Morgan in 'Ancient Society' gives the following list of Gentes of the Crows or Absarokas: —
  1. Prairie Dog gens, A-che-pa-be-cha.
  2. Bad Leggins, E-sash'-ka-buk.
  3. Skunk, Ho ka-rut'-cha.
  4. Treacherous Lodges, Ash-bot-chee-ah.
  5. Lost Lodges, Ah-shin'-na-de-ah.
  6. Bad Honors, Ese-kep-ka'-buk.
  7. Butchers, Oo-sa-bot'-see.
  8. Moving Lodges, Ah-ha-chick.
  9. Bear-Paw Mountain, Ship-tet'-za.
  10. Blackfoot Lodges, Ash-kane'-na.
  11. Fish Catchers, Boo-a-da'-sha.
  12. Antelope, O-hot-du-sha.
  13. Raven, Pet-chale-ruh-pa'-ka.

enemies, than when divided into small bands; though at such seasons as they are not liable to be attacked, they part for a short time. In general they are middle size men, but many of them are tall and stout and some inclined to corpulency which is seldom the case with American Indian.

Such of them as do not make practice of exposing themselves naked to the sun have a skin nearly as white as that of white people.[2] Those parts which the women keep concealed are likewise white, but their face, breast, arms and shoulders are burnt to the common Copper colour of the Indians by the scorching rays of the sun. Most of those Indians as they do not so often go naked, are generally of a fairer skin than most of the other tribes with which I am acquainted. It is my opinion that the N.W. Americans in General were they to be brought up in the same manner that we are, and their bodies kept from the burning heat of the sun, would in a few generations be as white as Europeans. Some of them have the hair of the head entirely gray although young;[3] and though I enquired I could not find that sikness had been the cause thereof. They make a practice like the other americans of eradicating the hair from every part of the body except the head, as fast as it groes, and deem it unseemly in a young man especially to have beard. The old men when they grown careless about their person let the beard grow, and in other parts of the body. The hair it seems groes faster than they could pull it out.

They practice so little walking & running, using horses on all occasions, that they are not so swift in running as their neighbours the Big Bellys and Mandans. I saw more cripples and decrepid old men among them than among any other nation except the Big Bellys and the Mandans. It is said that the Sauteurs and Kinistenaux tribes send their enfirms and old to Kingdome Come to ease themselves of the trouble of attending the care of them.[4] These Nations,[5] however, do it not, their old and infirm are of very little truble to them. The Mandans and Big Bellys

---

[2] From the period of their first contact with the tribes of the Upper Missouri, white traders and travellers have constantly mentioned the comparatively fair complexion of these Indians.

[3] From and including La Vérendrye, all travellers in the Upper Missouri country have noticed this peculiarity. See Catlin, I, 94-5.

[4] Peter Grant, in his valuable account of 'The Sauteux Indians' (Masson, II, 307-366), says that they 'greatly respect their old men while they are of some use in society, but if, from extreme age or other infirmity, they become incapacitated to follow them in their encampments, they are then considered dead to society, and their nearest relations think themselves no longer bound to maintain them; in this case a temporary shade is provided for them, with provisions and necessaries to prolong their miserable existence for a few days, and they are abandoned for ever.' Hearne and Mackenzie describe similar practices among the far northern tribes. See Lewis & Clark, II, 145-6.

[5] That is, the Crows, Mandans and Minnetarees.

Francois Larocque

are sedentary and the Rocky Mountain Indians have so many horses, that they can transport their sick without trouble. Whethere they did it or not before they had horses I do not Know; besides their country abounds so much in Buffaloes and Deer that they find no difficulty in finding provision for a noumerous family, which is likewise the cause of their having a plurality of wives,[6] some of them have 8 or 10 and 12, but in such cases they do not all live with him some are young girls that are only betustted.[7] But by far the greatest part have only 2 or 3 wives; some have only one, and those reason upon the folly of those that take many wives, and say that it is impossible for them to live happy and quiet as their wives are Jealous & for ever wrangling. They are not so stupid as Indians are generally thought to be. They reasons justly enough upon such subjects as they have had the occasion to see and be acquainted with. They certainly express wonder and admiration when such things are shown them as they have no conception of, of such as Spy Glasses, Watches, &c., but that is certainly no matter of stupidity. They know very well how to make unadvantageous[8] bargain in their sales and purchases, and discover no little share of ingenuity in making their saddles, fabricating knives &c. out of a broken piece of Iron &c.

They have not that taciturnity common to the more Northern Nation; I have never seen them remain any time in their tents alone with their hand between their knees and not uttering a word; they are social are fond of Company and are lonesome when alone. In walking in their camp numbers of small parties of old men are seen smoking and chatting together while the younger are playing at diverse games or exercising themselves at firing at a mark and..... When a Sauteux or Assiniboine enter a strangers tent they keep down their head, or muffle it so in their Robe or Blanket that it can hardly be seen. These Indians never do it, they are bold & Keep up their heads in any place and say that it is a sign of having bad designs when one is ashamed to show his face. A few Fall Indians[9] that I saw are the same.

---

[6] See Catlin, *North American Indians*, I, 118-20. Peter Grant says that among the Sauteux, 'the generality are content with one wife, yet polygamy is encouraged among them, and a good hunter has commonly two or three.' Grant adds that the first wife claims a certain superiority over the others, and is generally considered by the husband as chief mistress of the family.

[7] Probably betrothed.

[8] Unadvantageous, presumably, for the other party.

[9] Atsinas. The name Fall Indians as applied to this tribe is first found in Umfreville's 'Present State of Hudson Bay.' See his vocabulary of their language opposite p. 202. Also Coues' Henry, II, 530.

The North West Indians have been generally greatly misrepresented by some Authors, they have not that stupidity & listlessness which is attributed to them and I am persuaded that a child taken young from among his parents might be taught the sciences and would learn them as eassily as any other. It is not out of bashfulness that the Sautaux etc. hide their face when entering in a strange tent, but they esteem it polite. When they begin to smoke or after they have smoked a few pipes that they uncover their face but the custume is in general with the young men than with those of a certain age.

Jealousy seems to be their predominant passion; many do not go hunting without taking their favourite wife with them. The consequence of infidelity to the marriage bed is often dangerous to the wife who is often killed or wounded & some times the paramour likewise, but the most common revenge taken by the enraged husband is Killing or taking the horses of the wifs galant, besides unmercifully beating her. They sometimes present their wife to a stranger for the night, but that is very seldom & is always for some interested consideration.

Like all other Indian nations the women do most of their work, but as they are not so wretchedly situated as those nations who live in forests the women do work here that is done by man among the Cree, Sauteux etc & yet have less work to do and are more at ease while the men are proportionally idle.[10] When hunting they Kill the Cattle and their wives who generally follow them skin the animal, and dress it while they sit looking by; they do not even saddle their own horses when their wives are present nor do they take off their shoes or leggings when they come in to go to bed. In flitting the women ride & have no loads to carry on their backs as is common among other nations though it is certain that had they no horses they would be in the same predicament as their less fortunate neighbours for though the men are fond of their wives & use them well, yet it is not to be supposed they would take a greater share of work than other Indians. The women are indebted solely to their having horses for the ease they enjoy more than their neighbours. They are fond of their children but seldom or never reprimand them.

[10] Duncan Cameron, in his Sketch of the Nipigon Country (Masson, II, 239-300), gives the following account of the daily work of the Sauteux women, and with few variations the same description would apply to the women of most of the other western tribes: 'Their women must, even in the severest weather, put up all these lodges, and cut all the fire wood, as a man would consider himself degraded by doing that work, even if he had nothing to do all the time, but he will sit quietly smoking his pipe and hurrying them in the work. The man goes off early in the morning with his medicine bag, his

François Larocque

They live upon Buffaloes & Deer, very few of them eat Bears or Beaver flesh, but when compelled by hunger; they eat no fish. They are most improvident with regard of provision. It is amazing what number of Buffaloes or other quadrupeds the[y] destroy—Yet 2 or 3 days after a very successful hunt the beef is gone. When hunting they take but the fattest and cut part of an animal and leave the remainder; but it is no wonder that in a country abounding so much in Deer of all kind & Buffaloes & where the inhabitants kill it with so much ease to themselves, being always on horseback, that their love of good eating should expose them to the danger of a temporary fast. As deer keep generally in the woods it bears but little proportion to the Buffaloes that are Killed, excepting Cabri a small Kind of Deer resembling the Roe which always Keeps in the open country.

The hunting matches are regulated by a band of Young men who have much authority causing them to encamp or flit at their pleasure tell them where there are Buffaloes & to go hunting, they prevent them from setting one after another and make those that are first ready wait for the others so that they may all go together and have an equal chance. Those that behave refractory to their orders are punished by a beating or their arm are broken or their tents cut to pieces.

It is generally an old Chief who conducts their business and causes his orders to be executed by those young men whom we call soldiers. Every young man enjoys that Dignity in his turn. There are generally 10 or 12 chosen at a time for that purpose, both the Conductor and the young men are chosen by the other Chiefs. As long as the conductor is pleased with the post he keeps it, upon his resignation another person is chosen. Their Authority does not extend to every thing they only regulate the great hunting matches & the encampments, in every thing else every one does as he pleases. They also regulate the medicin feasts. The Conductor as he is called never does anything of consequence without consulting the other

gun, powder horn, shot pouch, his axe and ice chisel and leaves the women to fold their covering, pack up and haul along every thing they have. It they have daughters, they give each a load in proportion to their strength, and their youngest children they carry on their backs tied up standing in a sort of cradle peculiar to the country and well wrapped up in moose or rabbit skins, with a blanket over the whole to screen them from the inclemency of the weather. The women must dress the leather, make and mend the shoes of the whole family, skin and dress all their furs, mend their clothes, cook, put up and take down the lodge, cut and carry home all the fire wood, kindle the fire every morning, dry the men's shoes and rub them quite soft before they presume to present them to their husbands in the morning. They must set and attend the nets whenever they fish, and generally serve their husbands even if they were doing nothing at the time, and themselves very busy.'

Chiefs, and it is in consequence of the resolution taken in Council that he harangues and acts. His tent is thrown down the first when the[y,] rise the camp, he goes fore most all the way (except a few young men who go far before as scouts) and pitches his tent the first, all the other encamp about him. Previous to their fliting he rides about the Camp, and tells them to throw down their tents that they are going to such a place & for such and such reason. Some of the Soldiers go far ahead and others remain far behind to watch and see if there be no enemies. When Buffaloes are seen on the Road and the[y wish] to hunt the[y] cause the people to stop and the old man harangues from one end to the other. When all are ready the hunts men set off and the body of the people follow slowly.

When a quarrel happens between two persons they interfer and try to reconcile them by fair mea[n]s (that is when they push their quarrels to far) but I do not know that they ever employed an authoritative one. Generally a present of a horse or Gun is made to the offended person, as the means of reconciliation, but there happen few quarrels, and they are generally occasioned by their wives and jealousy. The young men seldom hunt until they are married, their whole time previous to that epoch being dedicated to dress and parade.[11] A Young Man rises late in the morning, about midday he begins to dress & has not finished till late in the evening, he then mounts on his horse on whom he has spread 2 *fais* Red and Blue and in Company with his associates he rides about the camp, with the wing of a Bustard or Hawk before his face in lieu of a fan to keep him from the burning sun, at night he dismounts courts the women or goes to the place of rendez-vous and at day light comes in to sleep. The married men dress fine but when the[y] rise the camp on certain occasions. To please the females and attract their attention is the motive of the young mens attention to dress. They in their turn turn as clear and fine as they can to please the young men. I have seen courtship carried on in much the same manner as we do, whither it is their usual custom of wooing the girls before marriage[12] or not I do not Know as I could not get the proper information; but some attention & deference seems to be paid to the young females.

I do not know what they believe as to their origin or their opinions, more than they believe in Good and Bad Spirits, and in a Supreme Master

[11] 'It is remarkable,' says Maximilian, 'that the men are far more vain than the women, and the latter are obliged to be greatly inferior to the lords of the creation in their attire and adornments. A warrior takes more time for his toilette than the most elegant Parisian belle.' See Catlin, I, 112, on the Indian dandy.

[12] On Indian courtship, see Catlin, I, 120; Maximilian, II, 279; Harmon, 294; James McKenzie (Masson, II, 417); Peter Grant (Masson, II, 319.)

of life. A pipe is never smoked without the first whiffs being offered to the rising midday and setting sun, to the earth, to the heavens, to these the stem is pointed to the respective place they occupy and a whiff blown to the same quarter, then a few whiffs are blown to diverse spirits which the smoker names and to whom he mutters a few words and then the pipe goes round each person smoking 4 whiffs & no more. The pipe must always [go] to your left hand man, as that is the course that the sun takes. What they call spirits are quadrupeds or fowls which the[y] think act as guardians angels. They have no notion of spirits in the [sense] that we have it is certain, but the[y] believe that these are invisible beings who have the power to do them Ill or Good and to them they make their offerings. One thinks it is the Moon that watches over him and another thinks that it is a Bee or Mouse and so on. It is their dreams that cause them to worship one thing rather than another, but the sun, moon, stars, heaven and earth are of General worship & an Oath on one of them is reckoned inviolable. Their is not an animal, fowl, reptile or insect that is not worshiped by some of these Indians who think that the object of his worship can save his life and render him invaluable,[13] whether it be a [bee] or a mouse. Inanimate things, such as a ball & stone, etc., are likewise thought to be able to do good or hurt.

They have no representation of the thing they worship, as Idols nor do they pray at any other time but when lighting their pipes. They have great medicine feasts, but these they make only in the fall, and I had no opportunity of seeing them. They are not superstitious with regard to the pipe which is the object of their most sacred regard.[14] Numberless are the ceremonies attended on smoking a pipe of tobacco. The regulations common to all are these, the pipe and stem must be clean, a coal must be drawn out of the fire to light the pipe with, care must be taken not to light the pipe in the flames or ashes and none must empty the ashes out of the pipe but he that filled or lighted it. There being but little fire I once lighted the pipe in the Ashes. My Landlord told me a few days after that his eyes were sore and my lighting the pipe in the ashes was the occasion thereof. Some will not smoke if the pipe has touched grass, another if there are women in the tent, if there are guns, if shoes are seen when smoking, if a part of wearing apparels be thrown over the pipe, if some one blows in the pipe stem to clean it, if the pipe pass over *Assichimous*. Some

---

[13] This should perhaps have been 'invulnerable.'
[14] Meaning not quite clear.

will not allow the stem before the Door, another must empty the ashes on Cowdung brought in on purpose, another again will not smoke unless every smoker be naked and none but smokers are allowed to remain in the tent, to one the pipe must be given the stem foremost, to another the reverse, another will not take it unless you push it to him as hard as you can, to some it must be given quite slowly. In short every man has his particular way of smoking from which it seems he has vowed never to swerve and cause to be attended by those with whom he smokes or he would think himself under the displeasure of that invincible thing (his guardian angel) and incur its resentment, he therefore in such case does pennance. A pair of leggings were thrown over a pipe stem, a person present whose [vow] forbade any such doings in his presence had the contents of the stem which was full of tobacco juice blown in his mouth & he swallowed it; the potion he took was so disagreeable that he was near fainting but he attributed his weakness to anger of the Deity that had been offended. Some who are to ceremonious in their smoking do not smoke but with their intimates and those that are well acquainted with their mummery; those that are less so take care to sit next to a man that Knows in what manner the pipe is to be given to them. The women never smoke. Before the smoking begin, he that has some peculiarity in his way of smoking tells in what manner it is, and every one attends to.

Their Doctors perform their cure by the application of simples with very few of which they are acquainted and by blowing on the afflicted part, smoking and singing, they likewise burn the leaves of Fir trees on some coals, the phisician spreads his hand over the wound as close as possible without touching it. Internally they have purging Roots which they take, and prepare some other, but as none was sick while I was with them I had no opportunity of seeing them perform any cure of consequence. They appear to be a healthy people. They have no other tame animals but Dogs and horses, few of the former but many of the latter whom they use on all occasions, for war and for hunting, they have them in trade from the flat head Indians[15] in great numbers and very cheap. They sell part to the Big Bellys and Mandans at double the price they purchase them and carry a continual trade in that manner. They had as yet given no Guns or ammunition to the Flat head Indians in exchange of horses, but this year as they have plenty they intend giving them some.

[15] Flathead Indians, of whom Larocque has something to say later. The name was applied rather loosely to several different tribes whose homes were west of the Rocky Mountains.

François Larocque

He is reckoned a poor man that has not 10 horses in the spring before the trade at the Missouri takes place and many have 30 or 40, every body rides, men, women & children. The female ride astride as the men do. A child that is too young to keep his saddle is tied to it, and a small whip is tied to his wrist, he whips away and gallops or trots the whole day if occasion requires. Their saddles are so made as to prevent falling either backwards or forwards,[16] the hind part reaching as high as between the shoulders and the fore part of the breast. The women saddles are more especially so. Those of the men are not quite so high, and many use saddles such as the Canadians make in the N.W. Country.

They are excellent riders, being trained to it from their infancy. In war or hunting if they mean to exert their horses to the utmost the[y] ride without a saddle. In their whelings and evolutions they often are not seen, having only a leg on the horse back and clasping the horse with their arms around his neck, on the side opposite to where the enemy is. Most of their horses can be guided to any place without bridle, only by leaning to one side or the other they turn immediately to the side on which you lean, and will not bear turning until you resume a direct posture. They are very fond of their horses and take good care of them; as soon as a horse has a sore back he is not used until he is healed; no price will induce a man to part with a favorite horse on whom he places confidence for security either in attack or flight.

They say that no equal number of other Indians can beat them on horseback, but that on foot they are not capable to cope with those nations who have no horses. They pass for brave and courageous among their neighbours. They seldom go to war, or to steal horses, but defend themselves with courage when attacked. They Keep an excellent look out and have always Young men night and day at 2 or 3 miles from the Camp upon the watch, besides they often send parties of young men on a two or three days scout on the road they intend to take. Any person of any nation going to their Camp will be well treated and received, but when coming at night or seen skulking about need not expect mercy. They cut and hash to pieces their enemies slain in battle but do not eat them. The young men and children seeks the Blood and plays with the Carcass, but I have not seen any Chief or respectable person meddle with the dead bodies. On the day they have got a scalp and the two ensuing ones they dance in the evenings. Their scalp dance is as follows, as I saw them dancing it when

[16] Either Spanish saddles, obtained from the south, or native saddles patterned on these.

they Killed two Assiniboines.[17] 17 young men, their face painted black and dressed as fine as possible stood in a demi circle singing and beating time with Drums and Shrisiquois or Rattles; before them 30 young women dressed in the war habilements of the men & carrying their weapons, their faces black danced to the music of the young men, 2 of them carried the scalps tied to the *Enclosa Pole*,[18] they danced in a circle & while dancing they advanced slowly towards the Center making the ring smaller, they then returned to their former station and began again, and shaking their heads always in union with the music. There were soldiers standing out side of the ring to prevent the people from thronging to much on the dancers. About the middle of the ceremony one of the Chiefs took hold of the bridle of a horse on which rode a young man plainly dressed & led him in the middle of the Dancers haranguing at the same time, the young man had Killed one of the Assiniboines. The chief then led him out, and they danced again, the other person who Killed the 2 Assiniboines was led in the Circle in the same manner by another Chief and a little after the dance finished. At night a band of young men walked about the Camp singing they stopped at the door of every Chief and sang songs in which were rehersed the exploits of the Chief at whose door they were. These ceremonies continued 3 days. In the day time the scalps were tied to the bridle of horses on which young men rode singing & beating the Drums.

Their arms are bows & arrows, lances & guns when they go to war they take their medicine bags[19] at least the Chief of the party does, when they have found out their enemies & on the point of beginning the attack the bag of medicin is opened, they sing few airs but very shortly smoke and then attack. It is generally at the break of day that they fall upon their enemies when they are fast locked in the arms of sleep. One of the Chiefs has part of a magic lanthorn on which he reckons as upon his chief support. The figures that are painted on the glass he thinks are spirits & that they assist him, he never leaves them behind when he goes to war.

They are excellent marks men with the bows & arrow but poor shots with the gun, but they practice dayly of late years they have more ammunition than usual.

They have never had any traders with them, they get their battle Guns, ammunitions etc. from the Mandans & Big Bellys in exchange for

[17] See Journal, p. 40, Catlin's account of the scalp dance, I, 246, and plate 104

[18] What 'onclosa pole' means is not clear. Possibly an error in transcription. See Catlin's plate 104.

[19] Catlin describes minutely the medicine bag and its miscellaneous contents, I, 35-8, plate 18.

horses, Robes, Leggins & shirts, they likewise purchase corn, Pumkins & tobacco from the Big Bellys as they do not cultivate the ground.

Their Dress for Men & Women.

The men wear tight leggins, made of the skin of Cabri or other small deer reaching up to the hips and the end tucked in a belt or girdle, the seam is ornamented with beads, porcupine quills, horse and human hair dyed with divers Colours.

Their Shirts are made of the same kind of skin and are composed of 3 skins, 2 making the body and one the Sleeves, the skins are joint together in the shoulder only & the sleeves also which are left open under the pit of the arm; the neck of one of the skins hangs on the breast and the other behind they are guarnished on the sleeves with the same materials as the Leggings, and their shoes are likewise decorated in the same manner and are made in the manner of mittens having a seam round the outside of the foot only without pleat. Over this part of dress they wear a Buffaloe Robe on which is painted their war exploits, or garnished with beads and porcupine quills over the seam. A slip of Wolf or Skunk skin is generally worn round the ankle and is left to drag behind as they walk, bits of red Cloth are sewed to it. The skin of the Bears foot with the Claws the[y] wear on the breast with as many buttons as they can find sewed to it, 12 or 15 Bears Claws threaded and tied round their neck is also very fashionable.[20] Over their forehead suspended from their head are two skins of Coloured Beads, with a few Hawk Bells or buttons, a little horse hair stained yellow which dangles on each side their nose, on their head they wear a *Killion* feather belt of brass & tin. None of them are ..... those who have long hair gum them into 10 or 12 plat plastered over with white earth, except the end which is well combed. Those whose hair is not long enough lengthen them with horse hair which they gum to their own and divide in the same manner as the other. I saw one that had two large white horsetails gummed to his hair, that was a black as sloe, when he walked the hair dragged 2 feet behind him on the Ground, they are fond of long hair.[21]

The women's dress consist in a pair of leggins reaching to the middle of the thigh tied with a garter below the knees, they wear no hair in their ornaments, but the seams of their leggins are covered with blue beads (which is the kind they are most fond of) and buttons when they can have them. Their leggins are round like stockings and have no fringes as the

[20] Maximilian, II, 261-2.
[21] Catlin, I, 49-50.

men's, their shift or cottillon reaches mid leg and lower and are made of Elk skin, but the fine ones are made of two large Cabri or Mountain Ram skins, like the man's shirts the bottom or lower part is cut out into fringes and garnished with Porcupine. The skins are joined below as high as the Ribs where an aperture is left on each side to suckle their children. The sleeves are joined to the body of the shirt on the shoulders only and encircle the arm from the elbow to the wrist, the upper part of the arm being covered only outside, but part of the leather is left to flap down so as to hide the pit of the arm.[22]

Their Robes and shoes are likewise garnished, but the former are never painted, they wear no ornament on their head, paint their faces red. The Children of both sexes are dressed in the same manner as The Sex they belong to, the boys go naked till they are 8 or 10 years of age, not for want of Clothes, but to be more at their ease, but the girls never. Both sexes are very Cleanly, washing and bathing every morning in the river, and in Winter in the snow, they keep their Clothes always clean, and as white as snow, with a kind of white earth resembling chalk, with which they dayly clean their Clothes. This earth has not only the property of whitening but also clears leather & cloth of spots of grease and other dirt, it is an article they are never with out. A woman never sets the Kettle on the fire in the morning without first washing her hands, and the men do not eat without the same precaution.

They seldom wear breech Cloths, except when they do not put on their leggins, as their leggins are so made that if they had a waist band they might be called trousers. They wear shells and Beads in their ears, but they do not cut them as the Sauteux & Sioux.

One of them had the tail of a Spanish cow in his Medicin Bag, and when he intended to dress fine or went to war he would put it on his head. They cut their hair and scarify their limbs at the death of their Relations. They are fond of small blue glass beads that they get from the Spaniards but by the second or third man.

The low waters are Generally in September.

Their Language is evidently a Corruption of the Sioux[23] as is the Mandan and Big Belly's to which last it bears most affinity and resembles

---

[22] On women's dress, see Maximilian, II, 265; Catlin, I, 51, 204. Compare Harmon, 275, and Alexander Mackenzie, xciv, on women's dress among the Crees and other northern tribes.

[23] For references on vocabulary, names, gentes, etc., see James C. Pilling's 'Bibliography of the Siouan Languages,' p. 22.

in the same degree as the Kinistinaux does the Algonquin or Chipway.[24]

	Big Bellys	Rocky Mountain
one	Nowaza	ama té
two	Nomba	Nomba
three	Nomini	Namini
four	Tobas	Shobas
five	Kichon	Kichons
six	Akaw was	Akaw
seven	Shapois	Sapois
eight	Noobassé	Noobassé
nine	Noobetzapé	Amatapé
ten	Pirakau	Pirakau
100	Pirakau tié	Piraké sash
20	Noombau Pirakas	the same
	&c	&c
large	Eties	Se
small	Carishta	Casota
head	Auto	Austio
River	Amjé	Amjé
knife	Matse	Mitsé
man	Matray	the Same
woman	Meay	Meay
my child, male	Matijay eshié	Matsay sa
robe	Ituwjé	I saw jé

They make very expressive signs with their hands to person that does not understand their language, they often told me long stories without hardly opening their lips & I understood very well. They represent a Sioux by passing the edge of their hand across their neck, a Panis by showing large ears, a Flat head by pressing with both hands on each side their head etc.

[24] 'The Algonquian speaking peoples,' says Pillins, 'covered a great extent of country, perhaps, than those of any other of the linguistic stocks of North America, stretching from Labrador to the Rocky Mountains, and from the Churchill River of Hudson Bay to Pamlico Sound in North Carolina.' Preface to 'Bibliography of the Algonquian Languages.'

[25] Maximilian gives the following, in his Vocabulary of the 'Minnitarris or Grosventres': — one, *nowassa*; two, *duupa*; three, nahwi; four, *tohpa*; five, *kechu*; six, *akahua*; seven, *schachpu*. It will be seen that, with the exception of two, Larocque's vocabulary corresponds pretty closely with that of Maximilian. Maximilian does not include the numerals in his vocabulary of the Crow language.

All the animals in their country are the following

Buffaloes	Fallo Deer or	Kitts[28]
Bears	Chevreuil	a few Foxes
Beavers	of both kinds	a Kind of Tiger
a few Otters	White Bektails[27]	(which I suppose is
Elk Deer	Vid: (a) below	the pant[h]er like
Cabri		that of the Alle-
Large Horned Ani-		gany Mountains)[29]
mal[26]		

(a) this is a Kind of small animal who live in holes in the ground like Badgers, but assemble in very large bands and make a kind of village. Upon any disturbance they issue out of their [holes] and bark at what disturbs them with a great deal of virulence.[30] It is hard to get a shot at them as they stand upon the borders of their holes and jump in upon the least motion. When Killed they fall in their holes from whence it is difficult to get them out. Captain Lewis caught one by filling its hole with water & as it always rose above the water upon its appearance it was caught hold of and Kept all winter in a cage at their fort on the Missouri. It fed of flesh & roots, they are of the size of a Musk-rat and of a Greyish colour, numbers of them of their village are to be seen about the Missouri & some are 3 or four acres in circumference.

Of fowls along the River Roches Jaunes I saw a flock of birds like the Grouse, much larger having a broad [tail?] which is spread when flying.[31] I could not shoot any of them they were lying on the ground among herbs and I never saw them until they were gone and flying; the whole flock did not rise upon the flight of one but each went off as it was disturbed in the same manner as the Groners, or as we call them her Phesants.[32]

The Flat heads inhabit the western side of the Rocky Mountains at the heads of Rivers that have a S. Western course & flow in the western ocean.

[26] See previous notes on Cabri, and Large-horned animal.

[27] Prairie dogs (*Cynomys ludovicianus.*)

[28] Kit foxes (*Vulpes velox*), or, perhaps, coyotes (*Canis latrans*).

[29] Puma, variously known as catamount, mountain lion, American lion, cougar, panther or painter. Its range is 'from Canada to Patagonia, especially among the mountains.'

[30] See Catlin's graphic description of a prairie dog village near the banks of the Missouri, I, 76-7, and plate 42.

[31] Prairie chicken, otherwise, prairie hen, prairie grouse (*Tympanuchus Americanus.*) Inhabits the prairies, from the Saskatchewan south. See description in Lewis and Clark, I, 201.

[32] Pheasant, ruffled grouse, partridge, common to the wooded districts of Canada and the Northern United States.

François Larocque

The Ridge of Mountains that parts those waters with the Missouri can be crossed in two days and no more mountains are found to the ocean. They come every fall to the fort of the Missouri or there about to kill Buffaloes of which there are none across that range of mountains, dress robes, dry meat with which they returned as soon as the Winter set in. They have Deers of different Kinds on their lands and Beaver with which they make themselves Robes, but they prefer Buffaloes. They have a great number of horses which they sell for a trifle and give many for nothing. They say there is white people who inhabit the lower parts of the River upon whose lands they dwell from whom they get glass beads and a kind of small cylindrical stick like wampoon.[33] Those people they say carry on no fur trade. The Beaver these Indians kill are singed & the skin eat with the flesh. They spear both fish and Beaver with darts made of Deers horns, they live part of the year upon fish, which by the description they give of it I think is Salmon.

Whenever they get a brass Kettle from their neighbors they do not use it for culinary purposes but cut it into small pieces with which they ornament and decorate their Garments and their hair. Elk teeth are likewise very orna[men]tal among them and they will give a horse for 70 or 80 of them. They trade chiefly with the Ererokas and give horses & horn bows for such articles as the Ererokas get from us, the Mandans and Big Bellys. The arrows they make use of in war are poisenous and are much smaller than those they make use of hunting.[34] They generally fight on horseback & have 2 bows and 2 quivers full of arrows, with which they defend themselves and greatly annoy their enemies even in flying. They are expert horsemen. They represent their country as so very good that what fruit trees groes here as shrubs are there tall tree. They generally speak very low, their language is very difficult to be learned, none of the surrounding nations speaking it, it resembles the sound made by a number of small bits of glass shaken together. Their bows are almost all made [of] the horns of different Kind of Deers and of one piece. They never saw a Moose Deer.[35]

The Snakes dwell east of the Flat heads upon the same range of

[33] Wampum. See Franchere, 244-5. Probably Hyagua, a small shell obtained on Pacific Coast.

[34] Lewis & Clark's description of the bows and arrows and quivers of the Shoshones agrees with what Larocque here says of those of the Flatheads, except that nothing is said as to the use of poisoned arrows, nor have I been able to find confirmation of this elsewhere. (Lewis & Clark, I, 151.)

[35] The moose is not found west of the Rocky Mountains, nor is it known to have ranged as far south anywhere in these latitudes, in western America.

mountains and on the head of rivers that have likewise a southerly course. They say there is much beaver on their lands and that they partly dress with it, they are all on good terms with the Rocky Mountains with whom they carry on such a trade as the Flat Heads. This nation is very numerous & each tribe has different names.[36] The more southern tribes have dealings with the white of New Mexico from whom they get thick striped Blankets Bridles & Battle axes in exchange for Buffaloes robes and Deer Skins, but it is probable that this trade of the Snakes is carried on at a second or third hand and that they themselves have no direct trade with the Spaniards. One of their tribes has been destroyed and the remainder being about 12 tents live with the Rocky Mountain Indians who are at peace with the whole nation & from whom they get in trade a kind [of] sweet intoxicating herb which they smoke as tobacco. Their pipes are made of a transparent stone. They have horn bows & horses which they give in exchange of knives, tobacco etc. This nation as well as the Flat heads trade has yet no guns from the Ererokas but this year the Ererokas intend selling them a few as they have many.

From the following few words of their language it can easily be observed that they must be of a quite different origin of the Big Bellys and Rocky Mountain Indians.[37]

One — Shemits.	Far — Mawnatow.
Two — Wawk.	Near — Mush tits.
Three — Pa its	Good — tsanti.
Four — Waw tsouts.	Bad — tish tsent.
Five — waw ni kith.	I love you — Makaw makan.
Six — waw watch.	Come — Keman.
Seven — tawt souts.	Go — Mean.
Eight — na waw tsouts.	Run — Kech tan.
Nine — sheman doun.	
Ten — Toshamb.	
11 — Shemits shemandow.	
12 — Wawk o mandon.	
13 — Past o mandow.	

[36] 'The Shoshonees are a small tribe of the nation called Snake Indians, a vague denomination, which embraces at once the inhabitants of the southern parts of the Rocky Mountains and of the plains on each side.' Lewis & Clark, I, 445.

[37] The Shoshones were a distinct linguistic family of which the Snakes were one of the northerly tribes, others ranging as far south as Mexico. The Minnetarees and Crows were of Siouan stock.

François Larocque

20 — Wawk on torhamb.

The[y] call themselves Sho shone that tribe that I saw at the Rocky Mountains.

October, 1805.[1]

Upon my arrival at the River la Sourie I found Mr. Pierre Rocheblave[2] who was proprietor and Bourgeois of the Department in Mr. Chabilly's stead, who was transferred to fort Dauphin department.[3] I passed a very pleasant winter with this Gentleman and F.N. Lamoth[4] nothing remarkable occurring during the whole winter. I made a couple of trips to the Indian tents in the course of the winter and the remainder of the time I passed chiefly in reading as there were plenty of books at the place.[5] Lamoth went to take charge of Appell Fort[6] in the place of Poitras[7] who was going out. On the 28 Mr. Rocheblave left this place (very sick) for Kaministiquia.[8] Mr. Falcon likewise went out this year[9] and no Clerk remained inland but those that had or was serving an apprentiship at R.Q.A.[10] and River la Sourie, where I was myself with two others. I passed

[1] In printing Larocque's Journal, the arrangement of the original has been strictly adhered to, though it might have been more convenient to insert what here follows at the end of the Journal proper, before the 'Observations on the Rocky Mountain Indians.' Larocque returned to River La Souris fort, as stated at the conclusion of the Journal of his journey to the Rocky Mountains, on October 22nd, 1805. He now proceeds to describe briefly the incidents of the winter 1805-06 and the succeeding summer.

[2] Pierre Rastel de Rocheblave was one of the pioneers of the Northwest Company; he joined the X. Y. Company in 1801; signed the Montreal agreement of Nov. 5th, 1804, by which the two companies were amalgamated; and replaced the elder Chaboillez in the Assiniboine department in 1805.

[3] Included in the country about Lake Dauphin, in what is now Western Manitoba.

[4] Very little is known of this man, beyond what Larocque says of him here, and the disastrous incident described by McDonald of Garth, to be referred to in a later note. McDonald says he was of a respectable family.

[5] This passing remark of Larocque's opens up the interesting question of libraries at the fur-trading posts in the west, including the famous little library at Fort Chipewyan, on the far-off shores of Lake Athabaska, as well as others of which we get random glimpses in the narratives of the fur-traders.

[6] Rivière Qu'Appelle fort.

[7] Andre Poitras, who was in charge of the N.W.C. post at the mouth of the Qu'Appelle, winter 1804-05.

[8] This trip to Kaministiquia — or Kaministikwia, to adopt the spelling approved by the Geographic Board of Canada — adds an item to the very meagre particulars of Pierre de Rocheblave's connection with the western fur-traders.

[9] Pierre Falcon. See previous note. 'This year,' that is, 1806.

[10] Rivière Qu'Appelle.

the summer of 1804 at this place[11] and though Buffaloes were at a great distance we lived pretty well and I had greatly advantage over my neighbours the.....[12] in point of trade. This is the only place in the Assiniboine River where the ....[13] have a summer establishment so that Mr. Lamoth at R.Q.A. is without an opposition. Having very little to do I kept a set of books according to the station method of duble entry so as not to forget it, in this and in reading I employed my leisure hours. Messrs. Chaboillez, Chr Henry, Hess McDowell paid me a visit in the course of the summer and [went] to the Missouri,[14] they returned with men who had passed the summer there on a trading jaunt.[15] On the last day of Aug: a man [arrived] from Kamt[16] belonging to lower Red River Department which was not ready to leave Kam: when they sat off. At the latter end of Sept. the brigade for this department arrived under the command of Big Joh. McDowell[17] the bourgeois of my first year in this country who was then coming from Montreal. Mr. Rocheblave having heard at Caministiquia of the death of his Brother Noel went down. Mr. Macdonell[17b] continued [me] in the command of the fort being that in which I summered and gave me a Commis[18] Mr. Lamoth. This young man had done very well at

[11] Fort Assiniboine, on the south side of the Assiniboine, near the mouth of the Souris. The date may be a slip of the pen for 1806. Otherwise, Larocque is harking back for a moment to the incidents of two years before. He has just been describing what happened during the winter of 1805-06, and the spring of 1806, so that what he now says may have been meant to refer to the 'summer of 1806.'

[12] If the date 1804 is correct, Larocque's neighbours may have been either the Hudson's Bay Company, or the X Y Company, or both. If 1806 is right, the reference must be to the Hudson's Bay Company. Harmon says in his Journal, under date June 27th, 1805: 'Here are three establishments, formed severally by the Northwest, X. Y., and Hudson's Bay Companies'; and Dr. Coues adds further particulars as to these posts (Henry-Thompson, I, 298). As the junction of the Northwest and X. Y. Companies took place on Nov. 5th, 1804, (Masson, II, 482 *et seq*) Larocque's only trade rivals in 1806 would be the Hudson's Bay Company.

[13] The reference is now clearly to 1806, and the Hudson's Bay Company.

[14] Some confusion here, either on Larocque's part, or in the copy. The expedition referred to is Alexander Henry's Mandan Tour. He left Fort Assiniboine on July 14th, 1806, the party consisting of Alexander Henry, Charles J.B. Chaboillez, Allan McDonald, Toussaint Viandrie or Vaudry, Joseph Ducharme, Hugh MacEacan (McCracken), and a young Indian, Pautchauconce, Chaboillez's brother-in-law. (See Henry-Thompson, I, 304).

[15] Henry and his party returned from the Missouri, Aug. 9th, 1806. Charles McKenzie and James Caldwell, who returned with Henry and the others, are no doubt the men referred to by Larocque.

[16] *i.e.* Kaministikwia, or as Larocque generally spells it, Kaministiquia or Caministiquia.

[17] In Masson's 'Liste des Bourgeois,' &c., are included John MacDonnell, John McDonald (of Garth), and John Macdonald, all *bourgeois* or partners of the Company, but no McDowell, neither is the latter name found elsewhere in the literature of the fur-trade at this period. Probably Larocque's 'Big Joh. McDowell' may be identified as the *bourgeois*, John MacDonnell.

[17b] Obviously the same mentioned as *bourgeois* a few lines above, which makes it clear that 'McDowell' should read 'McDonell.'

[18] *i.e.*, clerk.

Francois Larocque

R.....[19] It seems that notwithstanding the junction of the two companies[20] and the resolution they had taken of carrying in obligation[21] of all the differences, quarrels etc. which the animosity of rival ship in trade had caused that the N.W. Comp, could not forget the Death of the villain King[22] which this Mr. Lamoth Killed in his own defence on the Sassratcheoin or fort des Prairie department, or rather Mr. A.N. McLod[23] being of those kind of men who can never think themselves forgiven by a person they have grossely injured, because they are themselves incapable of forgiving, and who will continue hate, illwill and offences to a person because they [expect] such from him themselves. This Mr. McLeod with some others having influence enough on Mr. McDonell made him promise that he would render Mr. Lamoth's situation as irksome and as disagreable as possible in order to make him leave the Country, they being hurt at the sight of a person who called to their minds the baseness of their proceedings towards him. Mr. McDonell then in order to effect their design & his promise gave no command or employment what ever to the young man, would neither see nor speak to him and sent him to pass the winter with me hoping that such treatment would effectually rid them of him. Mr. McDonell at different times expressed his sorrow at being obliged he said to use Mr. Lamoth in that manner whom he knew did not deserve it but urged in excuse the necessity he was under of following the Directions of his fellow partners & the acquittance of his promise. Mr. Lamoth bore this treatment with indignation but Concentrated within himself however not to a degree as to influence his usual good humor. He dispised too much the author of it (whom he thought to be Mr. McLeod) to suffer the thoughts to intrude long upon his mind. I found him an excellent companion and in the Course of time a friend. He rendered me

[19] Probably, Rivière Qu'Appelle.

[20] On Nov. 5th, 1804, as already mentioned.

[21] Wiping out, or forgetting, is the evident meaning.

[22] The shooting of King (James King is listed under the department of Upper Fort des Prairies and Rocky Mountains, in Roderick McKenzie's 'Arrangements of Proprietors,' Masson, I, 63) by La Mothe, near Fort de l'Isle, on the Saskatchewan, in 1801, is graphically described by John McDonald of Garth, in his Reminiscences (Masson, II, 25-26). There had evidently been bad blood between the two men, and La Mothe's defense was that he shot in self-defense. Larocque's fierce characterization of King as 'the villain' seems scarcely justifiable. McDonald, at any rate, thought highly of him. La Mothe was tried at Montreal and acquitted; or, as McDonald cynically puts it, 'he was of a respectable family and escaped.'

[23] Archibald Norman McLeod, listed as *bourgeois* in 1804, Masson's list. Se Coues' note, Henry-Thompson, I, 277. McLeod may have acted vindictively toward La Mothe, yet he could hardly have been as bad as Larocque paints him, for Harmon and other contemporaries speak of him in the highest terms.

all the services in his power and volunteered them every time, that the interest of the Company required it, which was very often in dangerous as well as disagreable trips to the Indian tents & often did the duty of a common engagé[24] to promote the interest of those who illtreated him. I was absent 22 days at one time from my fort, during which time I gave him the charge of it, although I thought it would displease the Bourgeois. I found every thing on return in the best order possible in short I had numberless obligation to him & we passed an agreable winter together. I had under me one Clerk and an interpreter, one guide who served as Cooper & Interpreter and 9 men.[25]   There was a Hudson Bay establishment on the opposite side of the River[26] in trading opposition, the master of which was named Thomas Vincent, he had 23 men with him, and a great quantity of goods. We entered into some agreements in the fall with regard to the Indians and the trade with them, which we inviolably Kept and which we found to be of mutual advantage.[27] My returns were superior to those of last year at the same place and superior to my neighbours but the utmost exertions were used by me and Clerks, we were few men in comparison to our opponents, had 22 women and their family to feed. The Buffaloes our almost only resource were at a great distance, the men being hardly able to bring provision in fast enough for such a number of mouths, and with that our Indians & .....[28] to watch and bring in, so that we were unremittingly and constantly on the go, but we succeeded in surpassing the expectation of our Bourgeois who thought that 50 Packs would be the utmost of our return and we had 55.[29] I wrote an exact Journal of every days transaction Kept regular account, and Knowing that I would not be there the ensuing winter I left the whole with a character of the Indians for the use of my successor.

In May I had the house and hangards[30] which were not of absolute an

[24] Or *voyageur*, upon whom developed the purely manual labour of the fur-trade.

[25] Alexander Henry, on his arrival at Fort Assiniboine, July 12th, 1806, says: 'Mr. F.A. La Rocque has this post in charge for the summer. There are here three laboring men, an Assiniboine interpreter, and 40 women and children, almost starving. There are no buffalo in these parts at present, and they have finished what pemmican was left here last spring. Everything here bore the aspect of distress and desolation.' Larocque's cheerful narrative is in rather marked contrast to this tale of woe.

[26] Brandon House, built in 1794, 'nearly or about opposite the mouth of Mouse (Souris) river.'

[27] Compare Charles Mackenzie (Masson, I, 327.)

[28] Horses, probably.

[29] Of the neighbouring post of Montagne a la Bosse, John McDonnell says that it 'turned out about 60 packs a year, mostly wolves and buffalo.'

[30] Magazines or storehouses. James McKenzie, in his 1799 Journal (Masson, II, 386), speaks of the '*hangard* which contains the ammunitions, high-wines, &c.'

immediate necessity thrown down and had them rafted to a place called Pine fort[31] (from an old fort that had been there in Mr. Robert Grants time) about 13 miles lower down the River in pursuance of directions from Mr. J. McDonell who had planed the erection of a fort at that place, and the demolition of the one where I had wintered. Kept all the men that I could spare at work in rebuilding those hangards and before I left the place all the property was removed to the new fort, and under cover. In consequence of Letters I had received last fall from the family I had determined upon going out [to] Kaministicoia at least, and perhaps thence to Canada according to the contents of the Letters I would there receive would influence my mind. Mr. McDonell wished me very much to remain as the young men that remained in land did not possess his entire confidence and the time prognosticated a hard and disagreeable summer to them, few men could be left with them and there was much work to be done.

On the 3rd June I left Pine Fort in Mr. Charles McKenzies' care and embarked with Mr. McDonell for Kaministicoia. The brigade with us, Mr. Lamothe had been sent off with a single canoe 3 days before with directions to wait for us at the bottom of the River Ouinipegue.[32] We joined Mr. Henry at fork of the Red River[33] and Mr. Lamothe at Lake Ouinipiegue—we all remained at Mr. Wm McBays fort[34] at the bottom of the River Ouinipiegue 3 days in settling the mens accounts unloading the boats and canoes, giving the canoes their proper loads for Kaministicoia &

[31] John McDonnell notes in his Journal, under date Oct. 11th, 1793: 'Arrived at the Fort of the River *qui appelle*, called by Mr. Robert Grant, when he built it, Fort Espérance.' Masson, I, 294; also 271. This, however, was not Larocque's Pine Fort, which stood on the north side of the Assiniboine, west of Pine Creek. It was built in 1785, abandoned in 1794, and was variously known as Fort des Epinettes, or Fort des Pins.

[32] Or Winnipeg river. *Bas de la Rivière*, was a familiar name in the palmy days of the fur-trade. The first trading post here was La Vérendrye's Fort Maurepas, built in 1734. It was the first of several, under the successive reigns of the NorthWest and Hudson's Bay Companies.

[33] Where the city of Winnipeg now stands. See Coues' exhaustive note (Henry-Thompson, I, 43-5) on various posts at this point, from La Vérendrye's day down to the historic Fort Garry.

[34] The fort was known as Fort au Bas de la Rivière, and is mentioned in the narratives of Alexander Henry, *the Younger*, Harmon and David Thompson. The latter calls it Winnipeg House, but the former name was that in general use. No such name as Wm. McBay in Masson's Liste des Bourgeois,' or elsewhere in the literature of the fur-trade. It is evidently an error. Possibly Larocque misunderstood the name, or it may have been incorrectly copied from his original journal. Wm. McKay is listed as *bourgeois* in 1804, and signed the Montreal agreement of Nov. 5, 1804, as one of the wintering partners. He is frequently mentioned in David Thompson's journals; and may be Larocque's man. Or possibly the reference is to Wm. McCrea, or McRae, listed by Masson as clerk in the Lac La Pluie department in 1804.

different brigades from English River[35] and fort des prairies overtook us here. I embarked in the same canoe with Mr. Lamothe. Mr. McDonell gave us a profusion of the best kind of provision the country could afford for our voyage. He and other Bourgeois in half loaded canoes well manned[36] sat off a head and got much before us at Kaministicoia, at Lake La Pluie fort[37] I found some letters for me from Mr. McDonell in which he empowered me to take every thing I wanted at the fort to make our voyage pleasant and comfortable that fort being well stored with every Kind of provision.

I left my companion Lamothe at the Mountain[38] being the last portage on the way to Kaministicoia, there was a temporary establishment here, and Lamothe was directed to remain there until a Brigade for Montreal was ready to leave Kaministicoia when he would be sent for. This was the last mortification the poor young man had to endure from his employers. We slept but one night on our way down and the next morning we all arrived at the Grand Portage Kaministicoia which fort had been built to supersed the establishment of the Grand Portage[39] which being

[35] This was one of the most important departments of the NorthWest Company, as may be seen from the formidable list of clerks, interpreters and voyageurs credited thereto in Masson's 1804 List. English river was one of the early names of the Churchill, given 'by or for Joseph Frobisher, 1786,' says Dr. Coues.

[36] The partners of the NorthWest Company, like the chief factors of the Hudson's Bay Company, travelled 'light' in their visits to the various posts under their jurisdiction. See Malcolm McLeod's note on 'Light Canoes,' p. 41 of 'Peace River.' Sir George Simpson, of the Hudson's Bay Company, always 'had the best of canoe-men, Iroquois, and any extra Canadians who could keep up with them in quickness of stroke (60 a minute at times) and otherwise be up to their mark in the work.'

[37] Fort St. Pierre, built by La Jemeraye for La Vérendrye in 1731, stood at the outlet of Lac La Pluie, or Rainy lake; but a still earlier post had been built on the shores of the lake by De Noyon about 1688; and another by Zacharie Robutel de la Noüe in 1717. The N.W.C. post, Rainy Lake House, was on the north side of the lake, a little below Chaudière Falls. See Coues' note, Henry-Thompson, I, 20; and Judge L. A. Prud'homme's 'Tentatives infructueuses de pénétrer dans l'Ouest avant La Vérandrye.' (Trans. R.S.C., Second Series, Vo. XI, Sec. 1.

[38] Mountain portage is mentioned by David Thompson, in his 'Journey from Kaministiquia to the West End of Lac la Croix, 1804,' vol. VII of the Thompson MSS, but according to his account, as well as the later record of S.J. Dawson, the last portage before you reached Kaministiquia was Lazy Portage. See Dr. Coues' exhaustive description of the Kaministiquia Route (Henry-Thompson, I, 217-218); and S.J. Dawson's 'Report on the Exploration of the Country between Lake Superior and the Red River Settlement,' for the Dawson Route, which for a portion of the way was identical with the Kaministiquia Route.

[39] This was a notable place throughout the entire period of the fur-trade, French and English. La Vérendrye when he set forth in 1731 upon his romantic search for the Western Sea, sent his nephew La Jemeraye over the Grand Portage to Rainy lake, while he himself wintered at Kaministikwia. Jonathan Carver visited Grand Portage in July, 1767; and Alexander Henry, the *Elder*, in June, 1775. The first trading post must have been built some time about the latter year. In 1785 it was well established; and in 1797 a rival fort was built by the X Y Company. The N.W. Company removed their establishment, in 1803, from Grand Portage to the mouth of the Kaministikwia,

within the American Territory was liable to subject its proprietors to taxes & Imports from the American Government which to avoid the N.W. Comp. abandoned their Establishment at that place and erected new buildings upon a greater and more convenient site at the entrance of the River called by the Indians Kaministicoia, which name means the River whose entrance is full of Islands and Inlets.[40] The bay of Lake Superior in which this River empties[41] is indeed full of large and beautiful Islands and so is the whole of the North Coast of that Lake. The vessels that sailed on that Lake can come at the very gates of the Fort, the River being deep, and there Load and unload.[42] Before the Conquest the French....had a fort and trading establishment at this very spot.[43]

[Left Lachine] on the 26th of April 1801, and arrived at the Grand Portage at the latter end of June.[44] From thence I was sent to Fort Charlotte,[45] and returned back. Some time afterwards I was sent to English River for wintering there. From this place I was sent to Fort Des Prairies and Red River, passing lake La pluie Fort, Assinibois River, River

where what was later known as Fort William was built. See Coues' note, Henry-Thompson, I, 6-7; and Sir Alexander Mackenzie's Voyage, &c., (1801), xlviii-lxii.

[40] Abbé E.F. Petitot, S.J., says that Kaministi Kweya means Wide river; the name has elsewhere been interpreted as Three Rivers. There have been innumerable variants in spelling of the Indian name. The first trading post was built here by Dulhut about 1678.

[41] Thunder Bay.

[42] The North West Company had several vessels on Lake Superior, at different times, carrying supplies to the great distributing point for the western departments, Fort William, and bringing thence rich cargoes of furs to Michilimakinac, where they were transferred to canoes for the long journey down to Montreal. In an anonymous Journal, among the Masson MSS in McGill University Library, the writer says, under date July 3rd, 1793: 'Stopped at Pointe aux Pins (north shore, Lake Superior) two leagues above the Sault. We found Mr. Nelson building a vessel for the North West Company to navigate the Lake Superior and to be called the Otter. She is to be launched shortly....The Athabasca which sailed the lake before her is to be floated down the falls of St. Mary to help the Beaver to bring the needful from Detroit and Mackinac to the Sault, which the Otter is supposed sufficient to convey from St. Mary's to the Grand Portage, and in return she takes a cargo of furs to the Sault when they are arrived from the north. Part of the Company's furs are sent round the lakes in shipping, but the major part goes down the Ottawa in the Montreal canoes.' Aug. 2nd, he adds, having in the meantime reached Grand Portage: 'Old Bazil Ireland the guide arrived with two Montreal canoes and brings the agreeable news of the Otter lying off Point aux Pins. Early next morning a boat well manned was sent to tow her up into port and to their surprise spied her behind the point a la Framboise after passing before the fort in the night with a north-west wind. It was ten o'clock before she anchored at the wharf having entered partly by sailing and partly by towing.' On Lake Superior, see John Johnston's 'Account of Lake Superior, 1792-1807,' in Masson, II, 145-174.

[43] Fort Gamanitigoya, Kaministigoya, etc. See Prud'homme's paper, already cited.

[44] What follows is a very fragmentary account of Larocque's movements from the time he left Montreal in 1801, to the date of his Rocky Mountain Journal.

[45] At the western end of Grand Portage, on Pigeon river, 9 miles from the post known as Grand Portage.

la Sourie Fort, Rapid River, River aux Bois Fort.[46]

    1802 X Y Comp.[47]

    1803

    1804

    1805. februar fort of Mt a la Bosse. When I arrived at the Missouri in the fall, 1804, I found a party of 40 Americans under two Captains Clark & Lewis who were sent by their Government to explore the upper part of the Missouri & N.W. Countries to the Pacific Ocean, they wintered at this place and on the 28th March 1805[48] proceeded on their voyage of discovery with 7 piroques having sent the boats in which they came as far as this place down loaded with all Kind of minerals, Roots, plants carcasses & skins of different animals, and many other things, which they deemed worth the attention of the literay world. I offered to accompany them on their voyage,[49] but for certain Governmental reasons they declined my proposal.

    The Mandan Village is on the Missouri 1009 miles above the Confluence with the Mississipi taking in the windlings of the River and

    in North Latitude 47:21:40

        Longitude

    West of Grenwich 99:24:45

    from observation of Captain Lewis and Clark.[50]

[46] Rapid river, a branch of the Assiniboine, now known as Little Saskatchewan. 'River aux Bois Fort' is probably a slip for River aux Bosse Fort, or Rivière Fort de la Bosse, as Larocque elsewhere has it.

[47] For an account of the origin and history of the X Y Company; see George Bryce's 'Remarkable History of the Hudson's Bay Company, chap. XVII.

[48] The actual date was April 7th, 1805. See Lewis and Clark, (Hosmer ed.) I, 189.

[49] 'Mr. Laroche, the trader from the northwest company, paid us a visit in hopes of being able to accompany us on our journey westward, but this proposal we thought it best to decline.' Lewis and Clark, I, 168.

[50] Lewis and Clark give the latitude of Fort Mandan, their winter quarters on the Missouri, as 47° 21' 47".

Index

COLOPHON

This edition of the JOURNAL OF FRANCOIS LAROCQUE *was printed in the workshop of Glen Adams, which is located in the sleepy country village of Fairfield, in southern Spokane County, Washington State. The Larocque journal had been previously printed in English by the Canadian government in 1912, and again, in French the following year. The Ye Galleon edition is somewhat expanded and includes some material not in the Canadian edition. The type was set by Miss Bobi Pearson using a Compugraphic 48 computer photosetter. The setting in 12 on 14 Baskerville on a 30 pica line. A few pages with side notes are on a 27 pica line. The page numbers are in 12 point Baskerville Bold and the running heads are hand set type, 18 point Bologna from the Stephenson, Blake Foundry in Sheffield, England. The paper stock is 60 pound Hammermill Opaque in a vellum finish. Camera-darkroom work is by Evelyn Foote Clausen, who also folded the sheets using a Pitney Bowes multi-sheet folder. The Larocque pages were printed by Robert La Tendresse using a 770CD Hamada offset press. Stripping and opaque work was also by Robert La Tendresse. General book design and letterpress printing in color is by Glen Adams. The indexing is by Father Edward J. Kowrach, who also supplied the research on Francois Larocque. Some typeset corrections were done by Miss Kristy Frisbie. Binding is by William Bosch of Oakesdale, Washington. To these persons I give my thanks. All typographical errors are included at no extra cost. This was a fun project. We had no special trouble with the work.*